Cisco Networking Essentials

A Step-by-Step Guide to CCNA Certification Prepare for CCNA and master networking concepts

THOMPSON CARTER

All rights reserved

Table of Content

TABLE OF CONTENTS

Introduction

Welcome to **"Cisco Networking Essentials: A Step-by-Step Guide to CCNA Certification"**. Whether you're just starting your journey into the world of networking or you're looking to deepen your knowledge and advance your career, this book is designed to guide you through the essential concepts and skills necessary to pass the **Cisco Certified Network Associate (CCNA)** exam.

In today's increasingly connected world, the demand for skilled network professionals is higher than ever. Cisco, as one of the leaders in networking technology, offers a pathway to network engineering through its certification programs. The **CCNA** certification, in particular, is an industry-recognized credential that serves as a cornerstone for anyone aiming to build a career in networking. It validates the foundational knowledge required for network installation, configuration, troubleshooting, and management, as well as essential skills like network security, routing, switching, and IP addressing.

Why This Book?

This book is not just a study guide for the CCNA exam; it's a comprehensive resource that combines theory, practical exercises, and real-world examples to ensure that you not only understand the material but can apply it confidently in any networking environment. Whether you're preparing for the exam or simply looking to strengthen your networking skills, you will find this guide both thorough and easy to follow.

In this book, you will find:

- **Step-by-Step Instructions:** Each chapter is broken down into digestible sections, with clear explanations and practical examples to help you understand networking concepts from the ground up.
- **Hands-on Labs and Practice:** Throughout the book, you will find hands-on exercises that allow you to apply what you've learned in a simulated environment. These practical activities will help you gain the skills necessary to configure, troubleshoot, and manage a network.
- **Exam Preparation:** As you progress through the material, you will encounter practice questions, case studies, and exam tips to prepare you for the **CCNA exam**. These are designed to help you identify your

strengths and weaknesses, ensuring that you are fully prepared on exam day.

- **Real-World Scenarios:** Each chapter features real-world networking examples and case studies that demonstrate how CCNA concepts are applied in different industries. From small businesses to large enterprises, you'll see how Cisco's solutions are used to solve networking challenges.

Who Is This Book For?

This book is intended for anyone aiming to pursue a career in networking or IT infrastructure, particularly those preparing for the **CCNA exam**. Whether you are:

- A beginner looking to understand the fundamentals of networking
- A current IT professional aiming to add Cisco certification to your credentials
- A student preparing for the CCNA exam as part of your coursework

This guide will provide you with the knowledge and practical experience necessary to succeed in your networking career and pass the CCNA exam with confidence.

What You Will Learn

Throughout this book, you will explore a variety of topics critical to understanding Cisco networking, including:

1. **Networking Fundamentals:**
   - Key concepts such as the **OSI model**, **TCP/IP**, and how data moves through a network.
   - Understanding of **IP addressing**, **subnetting**, and how to configure networks for efficiency and performance.
2. **Cisco Devices and Configuration:**
   - Practical knowledge of **Cisco routers**, **switches**, and **firewalls** including basic configuration using Cisco's **IOS CLI (Command-Line Interface)**.
   - Techniques for setting up **VLANs**, **routing protocols**, and **network security** features like **ACLs** (Access Control Lists).
3. **Advanced Topics and Technologies:**

- o A deeper dive into **dynamic routing protocols** such as **OSPF** and **EIGRP**.
- o Concepts of **Network Address Translation (NAT)**, **Quality of Service (QoS)**, and **VPN configuration**.
- o Emerging technologies like **Software-Defined Networking (SDN)** and **cloud networking**.

4. **Troubleshooting and Maintenance:**
   - o Effective troubleshooting techniques, including how to identify and resolve network issues.
   - o How to use diagnostic tools like **ping**, **traceroute**, and **show commands** to monitor network performance and security.

5. **Preparing for the Exam:**
   - o In-depth exam tips, including strategies for managing your time, prioritizing questions, and avoiding common exam mistakes.
   - o Practice exams and exercises to help you assess your knowledge and readiness for the CCNA exam.

How to Use This Book

The book is structured to guide you progressively through key networking concepts, with practical labs, sample questions, and troubleshooting scenarios included in every chapter. Each chapter begins with an overview of the topic, followed by step-by-step explanations, hands-on exercises, and ends with a review section where you can test your understanding. You'll also find exam preparation sections that provide practice questions and exam tips.

As you read through the chapters and complete the practice exercises, you'll be building both your theoretical knowledge and practical experience. Remember, networking is a skill best developed through hands-on practice, so make sure to set up a lab environment or use network simulation tools like **Cisco Packet Tracer** or **GNS3** to get the most out of the exercises.

The Future of Networking

As you progress through this book, you'll discover that networking is a continuously evolving field. New technologies and advancements like **SD-WAN**, **cloud computing**, **5G**, and **network automation** are changing the way networks are designed, managed, and secured. Cisco continues to lead the way in innovative networking technologies, and staying updated with the latest tools and trends is key to remaining competitive in the field.

Conclusion

The journey to becoming a **Cisco Certified Network Associate (CCNA)** is both exciting and rewarding. By the end of this book, you will not only have the knowledge to pass the CCNA exam but also the practical skills to thrive in a real-world networking environment. Whether you're aiming for a career in network administration, IT infrastructure, or pursuing more advanced certifications like **CCNP** or **CCIE**, this book is the first step toward achieving your professional goals.

We hope that this guide provides you with the confidence and skills you need to build, secure, and manage networks, and we wish you the best of luck as you prepare for the CCNA exam. Let's begin!

Part 1

Introduction to Networking and IT Infrastructure

CHAPTER 1

INTRODUCTION TO NETWORKING

Overview of Networking

Networking refers to the practice of connecting multiple devices, such as computers, printers, and smartphones, in order to exchange information and share resources. The goal is to enable devices to communicate with each other efficiently. Networks come in many forms, from small home networks to large, enterprise-level systems that support thousands of devices. They can be wired (using Ethernet cables) or wireless (using Wi-Fi and cellular networks). At the core of any network lies the ability to send and receive data, whether it's emails, website requests, or video calls.

Networks are built on a combination of hardware (such as routers, switches, and cables) and software (such as network protocols, which define how data is transmitted). Without networks, we wouldn't be able to enjoy internet services, business communications, or even perform everyday activities like using social media or online banking.

Importance of Networking in Today's World

In today's connected world, networking plays a critical role in how we communicate, collaborate, and conduct business. Here are some reasons why networking is essential in modern society:

1. **Connectivity:** Networks provide the foundation for all digital communications. Whether for business, education, or socializing, networks allow devices to communicate and share information across local and global scales.

2. **Business Operations:** Every organization relies on its network to run applications, access data, and interact with customers. Effective networking supports tasks such as data management, video conferencing, cloud computing, and more.

3. **Internet of Things (IoT):** As more devices become connected—think smart homes, autonomous vehicles, and health-monitoring gadgets—networking is the backbone that makes it all possible.

4. **Security:** A strong and secure network ensures data privacy, protects against cyber threats, and allows secure online transactions. Networking technologies

15

such as firewalls, VPNs, and encryption are vital for maintaining online security.

5. **Global Communication:** Networking enables instant communication across the globe. Video calls, emails, and instant messaging wouldn't exist without efficient networking technologies that bridge distances.

Key Benefits of Obtaining a CCNA Certification

The Cisco Certified Network Associate (CCNA) certification is one of the most sought-after qualifications in the networking industry. Whether you're a beginner looking to enter the field or a seasoned professional seeking to expand your skills, here are key benefits of obtaining a CCNA certification:

1. **Industry Recognition:**
   o The CCNA is globally recognized, validating your expertise in managing and maintaining networks. It demonstrates that you have the foundational knowledge required to configure and troubleshoot Cisco networks effectively.

2. **Career Advancement:**
   o With the CCNA certification, you'll stand out to employers. It can significantly improve your

chances of landing a job in networking or IT, such as network engineer, network administrator, or systems administrator. Many job roles require CCNA certification as a prerequisite or a preferred qualification.

3. **Increased Earning Potential:**
   o Certified networking professionals often earn higher salaries than their non-certified counterparts. The CCNA certification can help you secure positions with higher pay scales and greater responsibilities.

4. **Comprehensive Skill Set:**
   o The CCNA program covers a broad spectrum of networking topics, including IP addressing, routing and switching, network security, and troubleshooting. This ensures that you gain practical skills that are directly applicable to real-world scenarios.

5. **Up-to-Date Knowledge:**
   o Cisco continuously updates the CCNA certification to reflect the latest technologies and practices in networking. Obtaining your CCNA keeps your skills relevant and ensures you're familiar with the most current networking technologies.

6. **Foundation for Advanced Certifications:**

o The CCNA acts as a stepping stone for more advanced Cisco certifications, such as the CCNP (Cisco Certified Network Professional) and CCIE (Cisco Certified Internetwork Expert). These advanced certifications open doors to higher-level networking roles and technical expertise.

7. **Job Security:**

o Networking is a critical part of modern infrastructure, and skilled networking professionals are in demand. By obtaining a CCNA certification, you increase your job security in a growing and evolving field.

8. **Networking Community:**

o Earning a CCNA connects you to a global community of networking professionals. You'll gain access to valuable resources, forums, and networking events where you can collaborate and learn from others in the industry.

In summary, networking has become an essential part of how we connect and communicate, and obtaining a CCNA certification ensures that you have the knowledge and skills needed to excel in this crucial field. Whether you're looking to start a career in networking or elevate your expertise, a CCNA certification will provide you with the foundation for success in the rapidly evolving world of networking.

CHAPTER 2

BASIC NETWORKING CONCEPTS

Types of Networks: LAN, WAN, MAN

1. **Local Area Network (LAN):**
   - A LAN is a network that connects devices within a small geographic area, such as a home, office, or school. It typically uses Ethernet cables or Wi-Fi to allow computers, printers, and other devices to communicate and share resources like files and printers.
   - **Characteristics of LAN:**
     - High data transfer speed
     - Low latency
     - Typically confined to a single building or campus
   - **Example:** In an office, a group of employees may be connected to the same LAN, sharing files on a file server or printing documents to a shared printer.

2. **Wide Area Network (WAN):**
   - A WAN covers a much larger geographical area, often spanning across cities, countries, or even continents. The internet is the largest example of

a WAN, connecting millions of devices worldwide.

- o **Characteristics of WAN:**
  - Lower data transfer speeds compared to LANs
  - Higher latency
  - Utilizes public or private leased lines for connectivity
- o **Example:** A company with multiple branches in different cities or countries uses a WAN to connect its remote offices to the main office.

3. **Metropolitan Area Network (MAN):**

- o A MAN is a network that covers a larger area than a LAN but is smaller than a WAN. It typically spans an entire city or a large campus. MANs are often used by internet service providers (ISPs) to provide high-speed internet to businesses and residents within a city.
- o **Characteristics of MAN:**
  - Covers a geographical area larger than a LAN but smaller than a WAN
  - Can provide faster speeds than WANs
  - Used to connect multiple LANs within a city or metropolitan area
- o **Example:** A city's public transportation system might have a MAN connecting its operations

control center with bus stations, train stations, and maintenance facilities.

Understanding IP Addressing

IP addressing is a method used to assign a unique identifier to each device connected to a network. These addresses enable devices to find and communicate with each other. IP addresses are written in two formats: IPv4 and IPv6.

1. **IPv4 (Internet Protocol version 4):**
   o IPv4 addresses are composed of four numbers, separated by periods (e.g., 192.168.1.1). Each number can range from 0 to 255, providing approximately 4.3 billion unique addresses.
   o IPv4 is widely used in many networks today, but due to the growing number of devices, IPv4 addresses are running out.

2. **IPv6 (Internet Protocol version 6):**
   o IPv6 was developed to address the limitations of IPv4. It uses 128-bit addresses, allowing for a significantly larger address space (approximately 340 undecillion addresses). IPv6 addresses are written in eight groups of four hexadecimal digits, separated by colons (e.g., 2001:0db8:85a3:0000:0000:8a2e:0370:7334).

o IPv6 adoption is gradually increasing as the demand for internet-connected devices grows.

3. **Public vs. Private IP Addresses:**

   o **Public IP Addresses:** These addresses are assigned to devices that connect directly to the internet. They are unique across the internet.

   o **Private IP Addresses:** These addresses are used within private networks (like a home or office network) and are not routable on the internet. Common private IP address ranges include:

      ▪ 192.168.x.x

      ▪ 10.x.x.x

      ▪ 172.16.x.x to 172.31.x.x

4. **Subnetting:**

   o Subnetting is the process of dividing a network into smaller sub-networks (subnets). This allows for more efficient use of IP addresses and enhances network management. For instance, a company might subnet its network so that different departments have their own subnets for better organization and security.

How Data Travels Through a Network (Packets, Switches, Routers)

When data is sent from one device to another over a network, it is broken down into smaller units called **packets**. Each packet contains part of the data being transmitted along with header information, such as the sender's and receiver's IP addresses, and other control information.

1. **Packets:**
   - **Definition:** A packet is a small unit of data that travels through the network. It consists of a header (containing source and destination addresses) and the actual data being transmitted.
   - **Process:**
     - When a device wants to send data to another device, the data is first divided into packets.
     - Each packet travels independently across the network, possibly taking different routes.
     - The receiving device reassembles the packets into the original data.

2. **Switches:**
   - **Function:** A switch is a networking device that connects devices within a LAN and forwards data packets based on MAC addresses (hardware addresses of devices).
   - **Operation:**
     - When a device sends data to another device on the same LAN, the switch

reads the destination MAC address from the packet and forwards it to the correct device.

- Switches operate primarily at the **Data Link Layer (Layer 2)** of the OSI model and are efficient in managing data flow within a local network.

3. **Routers:**

   o **Function:** A router is a device that connects different networks (such as LANs to WANs) and forwards data packets between them based on their IP addresses. Routers are responsible for determining the best path for packets to reach their destination across networks.

   o **Operation:**

      - When a packet needs to travel from one network to another (e.g., from your home network to the internet), it passes through a router.

      - Routers operate at the **Network Layer (Layer 3)** of the OSI model and use routing tables to determine the most efficient route for packets.

4. **End-to-End Communication:**

   o **Process Example:**

1. A device (e.g., your laptop) sends a request to a server on the internet (e.g., for a website).
2. The data is broken into packets.
3. The packets are sent through switches within your local network and eventually reach a router.
4. The router forwards the packets to the destination network (e.g., the internet).
5. Once the packets reach the destination server, the requested data is sent back in packets to your device.
6. The router and switches forward the return packets, and the laptop reassembles the packets into the complete response.

In summary, understanding how data travels through a network, the role of IP addresses, and the basic types of networks lays the foundation for mastering networking. These concepts are essential for configuring, troubleshooting, and managing networks effectively.

CHAPTER 3

NETWORK TOPOLOGY AND ARCHITECTURE

Common Network Topologies: Star, Bus, Mesh

1. **Star Topology:**

   o **Definition:** In a star topology, all devices are connected to a central device, such as a switch or a hub. This central device acts as a mediator for all communications between devices on the network.

   o **Advantages:**

      ▪ Easy to manage and troubleshoot.

      ▪ If one device fails, it does not affect the rest of the network.

      ▪ Easy to add new devices without disrupting the network.

   o **Disadvantages:**

      ▪ The central device is a single point of failure. If the hub or switch goes down, the entire network is affected.

      ▪ Requires more cables than some other topologies.

o **Example:** In a small office, all computers connect to a central switch or hub, which directs traffic between devices.

2. **Bus Topology:**

   o **Definition:** In a bus topology, all devices are connected to a single central cable, known as the "bus." Data travels along this bus in both directions, and each device listens for data addressed to it.

   o **Advantages:**

      ▪ Simple and cost-effective to implement in small networks.

      ▪ Requires less cable than other topologies.

   o **Disadvantages:**

      ▪ If the central bus cable is damaged, the entire network goes down.

      ▪ Difficult to troubleshoot, as a fault in the bus can affect all devices.

      ▪ Performance degrades as more devices are added.

   o **Example:** Older network setups, like coaxial cable networks, used bus topologies, where all devices share the same communication medium.

3. **Mesh Topology:**

   o **Definition:** In a mesh topology, each device is directly connected to every other device on the network. This allows multiple paths for data to travel, enhancing reliability and fault tolerance.

- o **Advantages:**
  - Provides redundancy. If one link fails, data can still be routed through other devices.
  - Highly fault-tolerant and reliable.
  - Ideal for mission-critical networks that require constant uptime.
- o **Disadvantages:**
  - Complex and expensive to implement due to the large number of connections required.
  - Difficult to manage as the network grows.
- o **Example:** Used in backbone networks or highly reliable systems where constant connectivity is essential, such as in data centers or telecommunications infrastructure.

Understanding Network Design Principles

1. **Layered Architecture:**

- o Networks are typically designed in layers, with each layer serving a specific function. This approach allows for more manageable and scalable networks.

- o Commonly, networks are structured according to the **OSI (Open Systems Interconnection)** model, which consists of seven layers, from the physical layer (Layer 1) to the application layer (Layer 7). Each layer has distinct responsibilities in data transmission.
- o **Example:** Layer 2 devices (like switches) are responsible for forwarding data within the local network, while Layer 3 devices (like routers) direct data between different networks.

2. **Segmentation and Isolation:**
   - o Network design often incorporates segmentation, which divides a large network into smaller, manageable sub-networks (subnets). This increases performance and security by isolating traffic within subnets and reducing broadcast domains.
   - o **Example:** In a corporate environment, one subnet might be dedicated to finance, another to HR, and another to IT. This ensures that traffic within each department is kept separate, improving efficiency and security.

3. **Redundancy:**
   - o Redundancy ensures that if a component of the network (such as a router, switch, or link) fails, an alternative path or device is available to

maintain network operations. This is essential for minimizing downtime and ensuring high availability.

o **Example:** A redundant router in a critical network path will take over if the primary router fails.

4. **Modularity:**

o Modular design involves building the network in discrete, scalable modules. This approach helps to simplify network expansion and troubleshooting. It allows for flexibility when upgrading or adding new devices and services to the network.

o **Example:** A modular router with different card slots can be expanded by adding more interface cards to support additional connections or technologies.

5. **Security:**

o Effective network design should include considerations for security. This involves setting up firewalls, intrusion detection systems, access control policies, and encryption to protect data and prevent unauthorized access.

o **Example:** A network design might include segmented VLANs for different departments, with stricter access controls and firewall rules between the HR and finance subnets to protect sensitive data.

Importance of Scalability and Redundancy

1. **Scalability:**
   o Scalability refers to the ability of a network to grow and accommodate additional devices, users, and traffic without major redesigns or performance degradation.
   o **Why It's Important:**
     ▪ As businesses grow, so does their need for a larger and more complex network. A scalable network ensures that the infrastructure can expand to meet these demands.
     ▪ It reduces the need for costly and time-consuming network overhauls, allowing for smooth growth and flexibility.
   o **Example:** A company with a small network that expects growth in the coming years might invest in scalable infrastructure, like cloud-based solutions, software-defined networking (SDN), or modular switches that can handle future capacity increases.

2. **Redundancy:**

- o Redundancy is crucial for maintaining network uptime and minimizing disruptions. By having backup components (such as duplicate hardware, alternative routes, or failover systems), networks can continue operating smoothly even if one part of the network fails.
- o **Why It's Important:**
    - In critical networks, especially in sectors like healthcare, finance, and e-commerce, downtime can result in financial loss, security breaches, or even life-threatening situations.
    - Redundant systems increase reliability, offering multiple paths for data to travel, ensuring high availability, and reducing the likelihood of network outages.
- o **Example:** In a data center, redundant power supplies, cooling systems, and network links ensure that even if one system fails, the network remains functional. A redundant router can ensure uninterrupted service if the primary router malfunctions.

3. **Balancing Redundancy and Cost:**
    - o While redundancy is essential for ensuring network reliability, it comes with additional costs. Network architects must carefully balance

redundancy with budget constraints to design an efficient yet fault-tolerant network.

- o **Example:** Small businesses may opt for less costly redundancy strategies, like using a second internet connection as a backup rather than a fully redundant data center infrastructure.

In conclusion, understanding network topologies, design principles, and the importance of scalability and redundancy is key to building efficient, reliable, and future-proof networks. By selecting the right topology and applying solid design principles, networks can meet the current needs of businesses while being adaptable for future growth and challenges.

CHAPTER 4

NETWORKING MODELS AND PROTOCOLS

OSI Model vs TCP/IP Model

1. **OSI Model:**

   o The **Open Systems Interconnection (OSI)** model is a conceptual framework used to understand and describe how different networking protocols work together. It divides network communication into seven distinct layers, with each layer responsible for a specific task.

   o **The Seven Layers of the OSI Model:**

      1. **Physical Layer (Layer 1):** Deals with the physical connection between devices (e.g., cables, switches). It defines the electrical signals and physical aspects of data transmission.

      2. **Data Link Layer (Layer 2):** Responsible for node-to-node data transfer and error detection. It frames data for transmission and manages access to the physical medium (e.g., MAC addresses).

34

3. **Network Layer (Layer 3):** Handles routing and addressing (e.g., IP addresses). It determines the best path for data to travel across networks.

4. **Transport Layer (Layer 4):** Ensures reliable data transfer, error checking, and flow control (e.g., TCP, UDP).

5. **Session Layer (Layer 5):** Manages sessions or connections between devices (e.g., opening, closing, and managing sessions for communication).

6. **Presentation Layer (Layer 6):** Translates data into a format that can be understood by the application. It deals with data encryption, compression, and conversion between different data formats.

7. **Application Layer (Layer 7):** The topmost layer, where end-user applications (e.g., web browsers, email clients) interact with the network. It includes protocols like HTTP, FTP, and DNS.

2. **TCP/IP Model:**

   o The **TCP/IP model** (Transmission Control Protocol/Internet Protocol) is a more simplified and practical model that is used to guide internet communications. It is based on four layers, each of which corresponds roughly to one or more layers of the OSI model.

o **The Four Layers of the TCP/IP Model:**

1. **Link Layer (Network Interface Layer):** Corresponds to the OSI's Physical and Data Link layers. It handles the transmission of data over the physical network and network access.

2. **Internet Layer:** Corresponds to the OSI's Network layer. It deals with IP addressing, routing, and the forwarding of packets across networks.

3. **Transport Layer:** Corresponds to the OSI's Transport layer. It ensures reliable communication and error checking, typically using TCP and UDP.

4. **Application Layer:** Corresponds to the OSI's Session, Presentation, and Application layers. It provides application-specific communication (e.g., HTTP, FTP, SMTP).

o **Comparison:**

- The OSI model is more theoretical, with a clear separation of each layer's functions. It is often used for educational purposes and understanding the complete networking process.
- The TCP/IP model is more practical and aligns directly with real-world networking, especially internet communication, where most of the protocols and technologies in use today are based on it.

Layers of the OSI Model Explained with Real-World Examples

1. **Physical Layer (Layer 1):**
   o **Role:** Defines the hardware elements of the network, such as cables, switches, and routers. It also includes the electrical signals that represent data as it travels through the network medium.
   o **Real-World Example:** The Ethernet cables you plug into your computer or router represent the physical layer. These cables carry the data in the form of electrical signals or light pulses (in fiber optics).

2. **Data Link Layer (Layer 2):**
   o **Role:** Provides reliable data transfer between two devices within the same network. It handles error

detection and correction, as well as framing data into chunks.

- o **Real-World Example:** When you connect to a Wi-Fi network, your laptop communicates with the router using MAC (Media Access Control) addresses. This communication happens at the data link layer, ensuring data is sent without errors.

3. **Network Layer (Layer 3):**
   - o **Role:** This layer is responsible for routing packets across multiple networks and devices. It uses IP addresses to identify source and destination addresses and determines the best path for data.
   - o **Real-World Example:** When you type a website's address (e.g., www.example.com) into your browser, the Network layer (using the IP address) routes the request through various networks until it reaches the server hosting the website.

4. **Transport Layer (Layer 4):**
   - o **Role:** Ensures that data is transferred reliably between two devices. It handles flow control, error detection, and recovery. It includes protocols like TCP and UDP.

- o **Real-World Example:** When you send an email, the Transport layer ensures that the email is correctly delivered to the recipient's email server. If any part of the email is lost during transmission, the transport layer ensures it's retransmitted.

5. **Session Layer (Layer 5):**

- o **Role:** Manages the sessions or connections between two devices. It ensures that sessions are properly established, maintained, and terminated.

- o **Real-World Example:** In a video conference, the session layer manages the establishment and termination of the session. It makes sure both sides stay in sync during the call, enabling smooth communication.

6. **Presentation Layer (Layer 6):**

- o **Role:** Translates data into a format that is readable by the application. It is responsible for encryption, compression, and data translation.

- o **Real-World Example:** When you download a compressed ZIP file from the internet, the presentation layer ensures that the file is unpacked into its original form so you can use it.

7. **Application Layer (Layer 7):**

- o **Role:** The topmost layer, where applications interact with the network. It provides network services directly to end-user applications, such as email or file sharing.

- o **Real-World Example:** When you visit a website, your web browser uses HTTP (Hypertext Transfer Protocol) to communicate with the server, which operates at the application layer. Similarly, email clients use SMTP (Simple Mail Transfer Protocol) to send emails.

Introduction to Networking Protocols (TCP, UDP, HTTP, DNS)

1. Transmission Control Protocol (TCP):

- o **Definition:** TCP is a connection-oriented protocol used to establish a reliable connection between two devices. It ensures that data is delivered in order and retransmits lost packets.

- o **Real-World Example:** When you download a file, TCP ensures that the file is transferred accurately. If any part of the file is lost, TCP requests the retransmission of that data.

2. User Datagram Protocol (UDP):

- o **Definition:** UDP is a connectionless protocol that sends data packets without establishing a connection first. It does not guarantee delivery, making it faster than TCP but less reliable.

- o **Real-World Example:** Streaming video or online gaming often uses UDP. These applications prioritize speed and can tolerate small losses of data without major issues, making UDP an ideal choice for real-time communications.

3. **Hypertext Transfer Protocol (HTTP):**
   o **Definition:** HTTP is an application layer protocol used to request and transfer web pages and other resources over the internet. It operates over TCP, ensuring that web content is delivered reliably.
   o **Real-World Example:** When you access a website, your browser sends an HTTP request to the web server. The server responds with the requested webpage (HTML, images, etc.).

4. **Domain Name System (DNS):**
   o **Definition:** DNS is a protocol used to translate human-readable domain names (like www.example.com) into IP addresses, which computers use to identify each other on the network.
   o **Real-World Example:** When you type a website's address into your browser, DNS translates that domain name into an IP address, allowing your computer to locate and connect to the appropriate server.

In summary, understanding the OSI and TCP/IP models, along with key networking protocols, is essential for anyone working with or studying computer networks. The OSI model helps break down the complexities of network communication, while the TCP/IP model provides a more practical framework for real-world applications. By understanding these models and protocols, you can build a solid foundation for network design, configuration, and troubleshooting.

Part 2

Cisco Devices and Configuration

CHAPTER 5

CISCO ROUTERS AND SWITCHES

Functions of Routers and Switches

1. **Routers:**

   o **Function:** Routers are devices that forward data between different networks. They are responsible for determining the best path for data to travel from one network to another, based on routing tables and protocols.

   o **Key Roles:**

   - **Routing Traffic:** Routers receive data packets from a network and forward them to the appropriate destination network. They use IP addresses to determine where data should go and can manage complex routing tasks across large networks, such as the internet.

   - **Network Address Translation (NAT):** Routers often handle NAT, which allows multiple devices on a private network to share a single public IP address when communicating with the internet.

   - **Packet Filtering:** Routers can also be used to filter traffic based on security policies, such as blocking unwanted traffic from entering the network.

- o **Real-World Example:** In a home network, the router connects your devices (e.g., laptops, smartphones) to the internet. It forwards data packets between your local network and your internet service provider (ISP).

2. **Switches:**

- o **Function:** Switches operate within a local area network (LAN) and connect multiple devices within the same network. They forward data to specific devices by using MAC (Media Access Control) addresses, which uniquely identify each device.

- o **Key Roles:**

  - **Switching Data Within a LAN:** A switch takes incoming data packets, examines their MAC addresses, and then forwards them to the correct device in the network. Unlike a hub, which broadcasts data to all devices, a switch sends data only to the device that needs it.

  - **Segmenting Traffic:** Switches help reduce network congestion by creating separate collision domains for each device, which improves network efficiency.

- **VLAN Support:** Switches can support Virtual LANs (VLANs), which are used to segment network traffic into different virtual networks, even within the same physical network.

o **Real-World Example:** In an office, a switch connects all the computers, printers, and other devices to form the internal network. It ensures that when one device wants to communicate with another, the data is sent to the right device without wasting bandwidth.

Introduction to Cisco Devices

Cisco is one of the leading manufacturers of networking hardware, and it offers a wide range of devices designed to build and manage networks. Some of the key Cisco devices include:

1. **Cisco Routers:**

   o Cisco routers are used to connect different networks and route data between them. They support various routing protocols like OSPF, EIGRP, and RIP, allowing them to intelligently forward data across networks.

- o Popular Cisco router models include the **Cisco 1900 Series** (for small businesses) and the **Cisco ASR 1000 Series** (for service providers and enterprise-level organizations).

2. **Cisco Switches:**
   - o Cisco switches are used to connect devices within a network. They are available in different models based on the size and needs of the network, from small businesses to large data centers.
   - o Cisco offers managed and unmanaged switches. **Managed switches** allow for advanced configuration, monitoring, and management, while **unmanaged switches** are more basic and offer plug-and-play functionality.
   - o Examples of Cisco switches include the **Catalyst Series** (for enterprise networks) and the **Nexus Series** (designed for data centers).

3. **Cisco Access Points (APs):**
   - o Cisco APs are used to extend wireless networks by providing Wi-Fi connectivity to devices. Cisco offers a range of wireless access points with various features, such as the **Cisco Aironet Series**, which provides high-performance Wi-Fi for offices and public spaces.

4. **Cisco Firewalls:**

- o Cisco firewalls provide security by controlling incoming and outgoing network traffic based on security rules. They are essential for protecting networks from unauthorized access and attacks.
- o Cisco's **ASA (Adaptive Security Appliance)** and **Firepower Series** firewalls are designed to protect enterprise networks from threats.

5. **Cisco Adaptive Security Appliance (ASA):**
   - o Cisco ASA combines firewall, VPN, and intrusion prevention functionality in a single device, offering robust security for both small businesses and large organizations.

Basic Device Configuration Using Cisco's IOS

Cisco devices use **Cisco Internetwork Operating System (IOS)** for configuration and management. IOS is a command-line interface (CLI) that allows network administrators to configure devices such as routers and switches.

1. **Accessing Cisco Devices:**
   - o To configure Cisco devices, you first need to establish a connection to the device. You can connect to the device using a **console cable** and

access the CLI through a terminal emulation program like **PuTTY** or **Tera Term**.

o Once connected, you will see the device prompt, which typically looks like this for a router: `Router>`. To enter configuration mode, type `enable` and then `configure terminal`.

2. Basic Commands for Configuration:

o **Setting   Hostname:** To assign a name to the device:

```
arduino
```

```
Router(config)# hostname MyRouter
```

o **Configuring an IP Address:** To assign an IP address to an interface (e.g., GigabitEthernet 0/0):

```
arduino
```

```
Router(config)#            interface
gigabitEthernet 0/0
Router(config-if)#   ip   address
192.168.1.1 255.255.255.0
Router(config-if)# no shutdown
```

o **Setting a Password:** To set a password for accessing privileged EXEC mode:

```
arduino
```

```
Router(config)#    enable    secret
mypassword
```

o **Configuring an Interface:** For setting up a router interface:

```
arduino
```

```
Router(config)#            interface
gigabitEthernet 0/1
Router(config-if)#    ip    address
192.168.2.1 255.255.255.0
Router(config-if)# no shutdown
```

o **Saving Configuration:** After making changes, it's important to save them so they are retained after a reboot:

```
arduino
```

```
Router# write memory
```

3. **Basic Troubleshooting:**

o **Checking Interface Status:** To check the status of the interfaces:

```
kotlin
```

```
Router# show ip interface brief
```

- o **Checking Routing Table:** To view the routing table:

```
arduino
```

```
Router# show ip route
```

- o **Testing   Connectivity:** Use the `ping` command to test connectivity between devices:

```
arduino
```

```
Router# ping 192.168.1.2
```

4. **VLAN Configuration on Switches:**
   - o Cisco switches allow for the creation of Virtual Local Area Networks (VLANs) to segment network traffic. Here's how to create a VLAN:

```
arduino
```

```
Switch(config)# vlan 10
Switch(config-vlan)# name Marketing
```

- o **Assigning Ports to VLANs:** To assign specific ports to a VLAN:

arduino

```
Switch(config)#    interface    range
fastEthernet 0/1 - 24
Switch(config-if-range)#  switchport
mode access
Switch(config-if-range)#  switchport
access vlan 10
```

- o **Verify VLAN Configuration:** To verify the VLAN configuration:

arduino

```
Switch# show vlan brief
```

5. **Saving the Configuration:** To save the configuration on a Cisco switch, you use the following command:

lua

```
Switch#  running-config startup-config
```

In summary, understanding the functions and basic configurations of Cisco routers and switches is crucial for anyone pursuing networking certifications like CCNA. Cisco devices are powerful tools for managing and routing data, and mastering their configuration through the IOS command line will provide a solid foundation for building, maintaining, and troubleshooting networks.

CHAPTER 6

IP ADDRESSING AND SUBNETTING

What is IP Addressing?

IP addressing is the system used to assign unique identifiers to devices on a network, enabling them to communicate with one another. These identifiers, known as IP addresses, are essential for routing data to the correct destination. IP addresses are essentially labels that are used to locate and distinguish devices within a network or across networks.

There are two primary versions of IP addresses in use today: IPv4 (Internet Protocol version 4) and IPv6 (Internet Protocol version 6). Both have specific formats and structures, and each serves the same basic purpose: identifying devices on a network and ensuring data is directed to the correct location.

Classes of IP Addresses (IPv4, IPv6)

1. **IPv4 (Internet Protocol version 4):**
   o **Format:** IPv4 addresses are 32-bit addresses, typically written in "dotted decimal" format. They consist of four numbers separated by

periods (e.g., 192.168.1.1). Each number ranges from 0 to 255, which represents one byte of the address. This format allows for approximately 4.3 billion unique addresses.

o **Example:** `192.168.1.1`
o **Address Classes in IPv4:**
  ▪ **Class A:**
    • Range: 1.0.0.0 to 127.255.255.255
    • First octet: 1–127
    • Default Subnet Mask: 255.0.0.0 (or /8)
    • Class A is used for large networks (e.g., governments, large corporations).
  ▪ **Class B:**
    • Range: 128.0.0.0 to 191.255.255.255
    • First octet: 128–191
    • Default Subnet Mask: 255.255.0.0 (or /16)
    • Class B is suitable for medium-sized networks.
  ▪ **Class C:**
    • Range: 192.0.0.0 to 223.255.255.255

- First octet: 192–223
- Default Subnet Mask: 255.255.255.0 (or /24)
- Class C is the most commonly used class for small to medium networks.
- **Class D:**
  - Range: 224.0.0.0 to 239.255.255.255
  - Reserved for multicast addresses (used for sending data to multiple devices simultaneously).
- **Class E:**
  - Range: 240.0.0.0 to 255.255.255.255
  - Reserved for experimental use and not assigned for general network usage.

2. **IPv6 (Internet Protocol version 6):**
   - **Format:** IPv6 addresses are 128-bit addresses, typically written as eight groups of four hexadecimal digits separated by colons (e.g., `2001:0db8:85a3:0000:0000:8a2e:0370:7334`).

- o **IPv6 Benefits Over IPv4:**
  - **Larger Address Space:** IPv6 provides a virtually unlimited number of unique IP addresses, solving the address exhaustion issue that IPv4 faces.
  - **Simplified Addressing:** IPv6 eliminates the need for NAT (Network Address Translation) because of its large address space.
  - **Automatic Address Configuration:** IPv6 allows for easier configuration of devices with features like Stateless Address Autoconfiguration (SLAAC).
- o **IPv6 Addressing Example:** `2001:0db8:0000:0042:0000:8a2e:0370:7334`

How to Subnet Efficiently with Examples

Subnetting is the process of dividing a larger network into smaller, more manageable sub-networks or subnets. Subnetting is necessary for better utilization of IP addresses, efficient routing, and improved security.

1. Understanding Subnet Masks:

- A subnet mask is used to determine which portion of an IP address represents the network and which portion represents the host.

- For example, in the IPv4 address `192.168.1.10` with a subnet mask `255.255.255.0`, the first three octets (`192.168.1`) are used for the network portion, while the last octet (`10`) is used for the host.

- **Subnet Mask Notation (CIDR):**

  o In CIDR (Classless Inter-Domain Routing) notation, a subnet mask is written as the number of bits in the network portion of the address (e.g., `/24` for a subnet mask of `255.255.255.0`).

  o **Example:**

    ▪ `255.255.255.0` = `/24` (24 bits for the network portion).

    ▪ `255.255.0.0` = `/16` (16 bits for the network portion).

2. Subnetting Example:

Let's subnet a network with the IP address `192.168.1.0/24` into 4 smaller subnets.

- **Step 1: Determine the New Subnet Mask**

- o Since we need to create 4 subnets, we need to borrow 2 bits from the host portion of the IP address (because $2^2 = 4$).
- o The original subnet mask is /24, so borrowing 2 bits gives us a new subnet mask of /26.

- **Step 2: Calculate the Subnet Increment**
  - o To determine the range of IP addresses for each subnet, we look at the borrowed bits. The subnet increment is based on the number of host bits left.
  - o A /26 subnet mask means there are 6 bits available for the host portion (32 - 26 = 6).
  - o The subnet increment is calculated as $2^6 = 64$, so the size of each subnet will be 64 addresses.

- **Step 3: List the Subnets**
  - o The new subnets will have the following IP ranges:
    - **Subnet 1:** 192.168.1.0/26 (Range: 192.168.1.0 - 192.168.1.63)
    - **Subnet 2:** 192.168.1.64/26 (Range: 192.168.1.64 - 192.168.1.127)
    - **Subnet 3:** 192.168.1.128/26 (Range: 192.168.1.128 - 192.168.1.191)
    - **Subnet 4:** 192.168.1.192/26 (Range: 192.168.1.192 - 192.168.1.255)

- **Step 4: Verify the Number of Hosts**

- o Each /26 subnet allows for 62 usable IP addresses (64 total addresses minus 2 addresses for the network and broadcast addresses).
- o **Formula for calculating usable IP addresses:** `2^(number of host bits) - 2`

Example for /26:

```
2^(6) - 2 = 64 - 2 = 62 usable IP addresses
```

3. Subnetting for IPv6:

- In IPv6, subnetting is much easier due to the large address space. A common practice is to use /64 for most subnets, which allows for up to 18 quintillion addresses per subnet.
- **Example:**
  - o Original address: `2001:0db8:85a3:0000::/64`
  - o Subnet 1: `2001:0db8:85a3:0000::/64`
  - o Subnet 2: `2001:0db8:85a3:0001::/64`

Summary: Subnetting allows network administrators to divide a large network into smaller, more manageable segments. Understanding how IP addresses are structured and how to efficiently subnet a network is essential for optimizing network performance, scalability, and security.

By applying subnetting techniques, you can make better use of your available IP addresses and create a more organized and efficient network.

CHAPTER 7

VLANS AND NETWORK SEGMENTATION

Introduction to VLANs and Why They're Important

1. **What is a VLAN?**

   o A **Virtual Local Area Network (VLAN)** is a logical subgroup within a physical network. It groups devices into a virtual network, regardless of their physical location on the network. VLANs are implemented on network switches, allowing network administrators to partition the network into smaller, isolated segments for improved organization and performance.

   o **Example:** In an office environment, the marketing department and the HR department might both be connected to the same physical network. However, by creating separate VLANs, the two departments' traffic can be isolated from each other, even if the devices are physically connected to the same switch.

2. **Why VLANs are Important:**

   o **Network Segmentation:** VLANs enable network segmentation, which can improve security and performance. By isolating traffic between departments or different types of devices, you reduce unnecessary broadcast traffic and prevent unauthorized access to sensitive data.

o **Traffic Management:** VLANs allow for better management of network traffic by controlling broadcast domains. Devices in different VLANs cannot communicate directly with each other unless routed through a Layer 3 device, such as a router or Layer 3 switch.

o **Improved Security:** VLANs can enhance network security by isolating devices or departments that don't need to communicate with each other. For example, sensitive financial data might be kept in a separate VLAN to limit access.

o **Simplified Network Management:** VLANs make it easier to manage and troubleshoot networks by logically grouping devices with similar roles or needs, regardless of their physical location.

Configuring VLANs on Cisco Switches

1. **Creating a VLAN on a Cisco Switch:**
   o **Step 1: Access the Switch CLI:**
      ▪ Connect to the switch using a terminal program like PuTTY or Tera Term.

- Enter privileged exec mode by typing `enable` and then entering global configuration mode using `configure terminal`.

- ## Step 2: Create the VLAN:

  - To create a VLAN, use the `vlan` command followed by the VLAN ID and name.

```
arduino
```

```
Switch(config)# vlan 10
Switch(config-vlan)#          name
HR_Department
```

- ## Step 3: Assign Ports to the VLAN:

  - After creating the VLAN, assign switch ports to it. You can assign individual ports or a range of ports to a VLAN using the `switchport access vlan` command.

  - To assign a specific port (e.g., FastEthernet 0/1) to the VLAN 10:

```
arduino
```

```
Switch(config)#          interface
fastEthernet 0/1
```

```
Switch(config-if)#  switchport  mode
access
Switch(config-if)# switchport access
vlan 10
```

- To assign multiple ports at once (e.g., FastEthernet 0/1 to 0/24):

```
arduino
```

```
Switch(config)#    interface    range
fastEthernet 0/1 - 24
Switch(config-if-range)#  switchport
mode access
Switch(config-if-range)#  switchport
access vlan 10
```

- ○ **Step 4: Verify VLAN Configuration:**
  - To check the VLAN configuration and which ports are assigned to each VLAN, use the following command:

```
arduino
```

```
Switch# show vlan brief
```

2. **Trunking Between Switches:**
   - ○ **Trunking** allows VLAN information to be passed between switches. By default, VLANs are

local to the switch, but trunking enables the propagation of VLANs across multiple switches.

o To configure a port as a trunk port (used to carry multiple VLANs between switches), use the following commands:

```arduino
Switch(config)#              interface
fastEthernet 0/24
Switch(config-if)#  switchport  mode
trunk
Switch(config-if)#  switchport  trunk
allowed vlan 10,20
```

o In this example, the trunk port allows VLANs 10 and 20 to pass between switches. The switchport trunk allowed vlan command specifies which VLANs are allowed on the trunk.

Benefits of Network Segmentation

1. **Improved Performance:**
   o **Reduced Broadcast Traffic:** In traditional networks, all devices on the same network broadcast traffic to all other devices. This can cause network congestion, especially in larger networks. By segmenting the network into

VLANs, broadcast traffic is limited to the devices within that VLAN, reducing overall network traffic and improving performance.

- o **Enhanced Bandwidth Utilization:** Segmentation ensures that traffic from one department or group does not unnecessarily impact the bandwidth available to others. Each VLAN can be optimized to meet specific performance requirements, ensuring smooth and efficient communication.

2. **Increased Security:**

- o **Isolation of Sensitive Data:** VLANs provide an effective way to isolate sensitive data from the rest of the network. For example, a financial department's data can be placed in a separate VLAN, with strict access control policies to limit who can access it. This minimizes the risk of unauthorized access and data breaches.

- o **Reduced Attack Surface:** By segmenting the network, you limit the number of devices that can access critical resources. For example, if a device in one VLAN is compromised, the attack does not spread to devices in other VLANs without additional routing or permission, making it harder for attackers to gain full control over the network.

3. **Simplified Network Management:**

- **Logical Grouping of Devices:** VLANs allow you to group devices logically rather than physically. For instance, devices in the HR department, regardless of whether they are physically in different locations, can be placed in the same VLAN. This simplifies network management, as network administrators can apply policies and configurations based on the VLAN, rather than managing each individual device.

- **Easier Troubleshooting:** When problems arise, network administrators can isolate issues to specific VLANs, simplifying the troubleshooting process. For example, if the HR VLAN is experiencing connectivity issues, administrators can focus their efforts on that particular VLAN and its associated devices, rather than sifting through a large network of mixed devices.

4. **Scalability:**

- **Efficient Use of IP Addresses:** Network segmentation through VLANs allows organizations to more effectively allocate IP address ranges. Rather than assigning a large block of IP addresses to the entire network, administrators can assign smaller, more appropriate subnets to each VLAN, reducing waste and making it easier to scale the network as the organization grows.

- o **Flexibility in Expansion:** As a network grows, it's much easier to add new VLANs to accommodate additional departments, projects, or devices. VLANs provide the flexibility to expand the network without needing significant physical changes to the underlying infrastructure.

5. **Better Quality of Service (QoS):**

- o **Prioritization of Traffic:** With VLANs, administrators can implement Quality of Service (QoS) policies to prioritize certain types of traffic, such as VoIP (Voice over IP) or video conferencing, over less time-sensitive data, such as email. This ensures that critical applications get the bandwidth they need, leading to better performance and reliability.

- o **Traffic Control:** By segmenting traffic, administrators can more easily manage traffic flow, ensuring that high-priority applications are not delayed or degraded by lower-priority traffic.

6. **Cost Savings:**

- o **Reduced Hardware Costs:** VLANs allow a single physical network to be used to support multiple logical networks. This reduces the need for additional physical network hardware (such as separate switches or routers) to support different departments or services.

- o **Lower Maintenance Costs:** Network segmentation can also lower maintenance costs because issues can be isolated to specific VLANs, making troubleshooting faster and more efficient.

Conclusion

VLANs and network segmentation are essential tools for modern network management. By creating logical groupings of devices, VLANs enable improved performance, enhanced security, simplified management, and cost savings. Cisco devices make it relatively easy to configure and manage VLANs, providing flexibility and scalability as networks grow. Implementing VLANs and segmentation best practices is critical for creating efficient, secure, and well-organized networks.

CHAPTER 8

ROUTING PROTOCOLS: STATIC AND DYNAMIC ROUTING

Difference Between Static and Dynamic Routing

1. **Static Routing:**

   o **Definition:** Static routing is a routing technique where routes are manually configured by a network administrator. The routes do not change unless manually updated. In static routing, the routing table is fixed and does not adapt to changes in the network topology.

   o **Advantages:**

     ▪ **Simple to Configure:** Static routes are easy to set up on small, stable networks with few changes.

     ▪ **Low Overhead:** Since there are no routing protocol updates happening in the background, static routes require minimal CPU and bandwidth.

     ▪ **Predictable:** Static routes are highly predictable since they don't change unless manually modified.

o **Disadvantages:**

- **Lack of Flexibility:** Static routing doesn't adjust to changes in the network topology, so if a link goes down, traffic might be disrupted until the route is manually updated.

- **Scalability Issues:** In larger networks, manually configuring routes becomes complex and impractical. Adding or changing network paths requires manual updates across all routers.

o **Example:**

- A simple network where two routers are connected directly with a static route. The administrator manually configures the route between Router A and Router B to ensure the two networks can communicate. If a link fails, the administrator must manually reconfigure the route to bypass the failure.

2. **Dynamic Routing:**

o **Definition:** Dynamic routing uses routing protocols to automatically discover and maintain the routing table. Routers exchange routing information, and the table is dynamically updated based on the network's topology and changes in the network, such as link failures or additions.

- o **Advantages:**
  - **Adaptability:** Dynamic routing adjusts to network changes automatically, so if a link goes down, routes are recalculated, and traffic is rerouted dynamically.
  - **Scalability:** It is more suitable for large, complex networks where routes need to be updated regularly without manual intervention.
  - **Less Administrative Overhead:** Routing protocols reduce the administrative burden because they automatically manage routing tables.
- o **Disadvantages:**
  - **Higher Overhead:** Dynamic routing requires more CPU, memory, and bandwidth because routers need to exchange routing information and constantly update their tables.
  - **Complexity:** Configuring dynamic routing can be more complex than static routing, especially for administrators new to routing protocols.
- o **Example:**

- In a large network where multiple routers are connected to various subnets, dynamic routing protocols like OSPF or EIGRP help maintain up-to-date routing tables automatically. If a router fails, the network adapts and traffic is rerouted without the need for manual intervention.

Introduction to Routing Protocols (RIP, OSPF, EIGRP)

1. Routing Information Protocol (RIP):

o **Definition:** RIP is one of the oldest and simplest dynamic routing protocols. It uses the **distance-vector** method, where routers share their routing tables with their neighbors to determine the best paths. RIP's metric is based on hop count, with a maximum of 15 hops allowed, making it suitable for smaller networks.

o **Key Features:**

- **Distance-Vector Protocol:** RIP routers share routing tables with neighbors, and the best route is determined by the fewest number of hops.

- **Hop Count Limit:** RIP limits the number of hops to 15, meaning that any route with more than 15 hops is considered unreachable.

74

- **Periodic Updates:** RIP updates its routing table every 30 seconds, which can cause network traffic overhead.
  - **Real-World Use:**
    - RIP is often used in small office or home networks where the network is not expected to grow significantly and where a simple routing solution is sufficient.

2. **Open Shortest Path First (OSPF):**
   - **Definition:** OSPF is a **link-state** routing protocol, where each router maintains a map of the network's topology and calculates the shortest path to each destination using an algorithm like Dijkstra's algorithm. OSPF is more scalable and efficient than RIP, especially for larger networks.
   - **Key Features:**
     - **Link-State Protocol:** Routers share information about the state of their links, which is used to build a network topology map.
     - **Cost Metric:** OSPF uses a **cost** metric based on bandwidth to determine the best path.
     - **Hierarchical Design:** OSPF supports hierarchical network designs using

areas, making it scalable for large enterprise networks.

- ○ **Real-World Use:**
  - OSPF is commonly used in medium to large enterprise networks, data centers, and service provider environments because it can scale effectively and provides quicker convergence times compared to RIP.

3. **Enhanced Interior Gateway Routing Protocol (EIGRP):**

   - ○ **Definition:** EIGRP is a **hybrid routing protocol** developed by Cisco, combining the features of both distance-vector and link-state protocols. EIGRP uses the **Diffusing Update Algorithm (DUAL)** to calculate the best paths and supports advanced features like unequal-cost load balancing.

   - ○ **Key Features:**
     - **Hybrid Protocol:** EIGRP uses both distance-vector and link-state methods, providing more flexibility and quicker convergence times.
     - **Metric Based on Multiple Factors:** EIGRP uses a composite metric that

considers bandwidth, delay, reliability, and load to determine the best path.

- **Faster Convergence:** EIGRP has a faster convergence time compared to RIP and OSPF, making it suitable for large networks.

o **Real-World Use:**

- EIGRP is often used in large enterprise networks, especially where Cisco devices are dominant. Its flexibility and scalability make it ideal for networks that require robust routing decisions and faster recovery in case of failures.

Real-World Examples of Routing Decisions

1. **Example 1: Static Routing in a Small Business Network:**

o A small business has two routers: one connected to the internet and one connected to internal devices. The administrator manually configures a static route on Router A to direct traffic destined for the internet through Router B.

o **Routing Decision:**

- Router A has a static route that says:

ruby

```
0.0.0.0/0    ->    Next    Hop:
192.168.1.1 (Router B)
```

- This static route tells Router A to forward all outbound traffic destined for addresses outside its local network to Router B.

2. **Example 2: Dynamic Routing with OSPF in a Corporate Network:**

   o A large corporation uses OSPF for routing between multiple branches in different cities. The network is designed with OSPF areas, and routers exchange link-state information to build a topology map. If one link between two cities fails, OSPF automatically recalculates the best route and redirects traffic through alternative paths without manual intervention.

   o **Routing Decision:**

      - If the main link between Branch A and Branch B fails, OSPF will quickly calculate the best path based on the link's cost, and traffic will be rerouted through Branch C, maintaining network continuity.

3. **Example 3: EIGRP Routing Decision in a Large Enterprise:**

- o In a large enterprise with multiple routers connected to various subnets, EIGRP is used to calculate the best routes based on multiple metrics. EIGRP can perform load balancing across multiple paths if the paths have the same metric but different costs, ensuring efficient use of available bandwidth.
- o **Routing Decision:**
  - Suppose Router 1 has two paths to reach a destination network: one with a lower cost (but higher bandwidth) and one with a higher cost (but lower latency). EIGRP will choose the lower cost path, but if needed, it will also distribute some traffic over the second path, optimizing bandwidth utilization.

In summary, static and dynamic routing both play crucial roles in network routing. Static routing is ideal for smaller, stable networks, whereas dynamic routing protocols like RIP, OSPF, and EIGRP offer flexibility, scalability, and adaptability for larger and more complex networks. Understanding the differences between static and dynamic routing, as well as the operation of key routing protocols, is essential for efficient network design and maintenance.

CHAPTER 9

CONFIGURING ROUTING PROTOCOLS (RIP, OSPF, EIGRP)

Setting Up RIP, OSPF, and EIGRP

1. Setting Up RIP (Routing Information Protocol)

Step 1: Enter Global Configuration Mode

- Connect to your Cisco router and access global configuration mode:

```shell
Router> enable
Router# configure terminal
Router(config)#
```

Step 2: Enable RIP and Define the Network

- To enable RIP, you use the `router rip` command. You then specify the networks that RIP should advertise.

```arduino
Router(config)# router rip
```

80

```
Router(config-router)# version 2
Router(config-router)#          network
192.168.1.0
Router(config-router)#          network
192.168.2.0
```

- The `version 2` command specifies that RIP v2 will be used (RIP v2 supports classless routing).
- The `network` command tells the router to advertise the specified network.

Step 3: Check the RIP Configuration

o To verify the RIP routing table:

```
arduino
```

```
Router# show ip route rip
```

Step 4: Save Configuration

o Don't forget to save your configuration to prevent it from being lost after a reboot:

```
lua
```

```
Router#     running-config    startup-
config
```

81

Key Considerations:

- o RIP is suitable for small networks but limited by the 15-hop count, which restricts its scalability.
- o RIP updates its routing table every 30 seconds, which can create network overhead in large or busy networks.

2. Setting Up OSPF (Open Shortest Path First)

Step 1: Enter Global Configuration Mode

- o As with RIP, begin by accessing global configuration mode:

```shell
Router> enable
Router# configure terminal
Router(config)#
```

Step 2: Enable OSPF and Define the Router ID

- o To enable OSPF, use the `router ospf` command followed by the OSPF process ID (an arbitrary number used to identify OSPF routing processes).

```arduino
```

```
Router(config)# router ospf 1
Router(config-router)#      router-id
1.1.1.1
```

- The `router-id` command assigns a unique identifier to the OSPF router.

Step 3: Define the Networks to Be Included in OSPF

o   Use the `network` command to include networks in the OSPF process:

```
arduino
```

```
Router(config-router)#      network
192.168.1.0 0.0.0.255 area 0
Router(config-router)#      network
192.168.2.0 0.0.0.255 area 0
```

- The `area 0` command assigns the networks to OSPF area 0, the backbone area of OSPF.

Step 4: Check OSPF Configuration

o   To verify OSPF routing:

```
arduino
```

```
Router# show ip ospf neighbor
Router# show ip ospf
```

Step 5: Save Configuration

o   Save the configuration:

```
lua
```

```
Router#    running-config    startup-
config
```

Key Considerations:

o   OSPF uses a link-state routing algorithm and is more scalable than RIP.

o   OSPF supports hierarchical network designs using areas, which helps optimize performance and reduce overhead.

3. **Setting Up EIGRP (Enhanced Interior Gateway Routing Protocol)**

Step 1: Enter Global Configuration Mode

o   Access global configuration mode:

```
shell
```

```
Router> enable
Router# configure terminal
Router(config)#
```

Step 2: Enable EIGRP and Define the Autonomous System Number

o To enable EIGRP, use the `router eigrp` command followed by the Autonomous System (AS) number (a unique identifier for an EIGRP network):

arduino

```
Router(config)# router eigrp 100
```

Step 3: Define the Networks to Be Included in EIGRP

o Use the `network` command to specify the networks to be advertised by EIGRP:

arduino

```
Router(config-router)#        network
192.168.1.0
Router(config-router)#        network
192.168.2.0
```

Step 4: Check EIGRP Configuration

o   To verify EIGRP routing:

arduino

```
Router# show ip eigrp neighbors
Router# show ip eigrp topology
```

Step 5: Save Configuration

o   Save your configuration:

lua

```
Router#    running-config   startup-
config
```

Key Considerations:

o   EIGRP uses a hybrid routing approach, combining features of both distance-vector and link-state protocols.

o   It is known for faster convergence times and efficient use of bandwidth compared to RIP and OSPF.

Examples of Configuring Dynamic Routing in Cisco Environments

1. **Example: Configuring OSPF in a Multi-Area Network**

   o In a large enterprise with multiple offices, OSPF can be used to ensure efficient routing across different areas.

   o **Step 1:** Configure OSPF on Router 1 and Router 2, each in different areas:

   arduino

   ```
   Router1(config)# router ospf 1
   Router1(config-router)#      network
   192.168.1.0 0.0.0.255 area 0
   Router1(config-router)#      network
   192.168.2.0 0.0.0.255 area 1
   Router2(config)# router ospf 1
   Router2(config-router)#      network
   192.168.2.0 0.0.0.255 area 1
   Router2(config-router)#      network
   192.168.3.0 0.0.0.255 area 0
   ```

2. **Example: Configuring EIGRP for Load Balancing**

   o EIGRP can perform load balancing across multiple paths to a destination, helping optimize bandwidth usage.

- ○ **Step 1:** Configure EIGRP and enable equal-cost load balancing:

arduino

```
Router(config)# router eigrp 100
Router(config-router)#        network
192.168.1.0
Router(config-router)# maximum-paths
4
```

3. **Example: Configuring RIP on a Simple Network**

- ○ In a small network with two routers connected, RIP can be used to handle routing between them.
- ○ **Step 1:** Enable RIP on both routers and define the network:

arduino

```
Router1(config)# router rip
Router1(config-router)#        network
192.168.1.0
Router2(config)# router rip
Router2(config-router)#        network
192.168.2.0
```

Troubleshooting Routing Issues

1. **Verifying Routing Tables:**
   - o To ensure that routes are being advertised and received correctly, check the router's routing table using the following commands:
     - **For RIP:** `show ip route rip`
     - **For OSPF:** `show ip ospf`
     - **For EIGRP:** `show ip eigrp neighbors`

2. **Checking Neighbors and Convergence:**
   - o If a routing protocol is not converging properly, ensure that the routers are forming neighbors. Check the neighbor relationships:
     - **For OSPF:** `show ip ospf neighbor`
     - **For EIGRP:** `show ip eigrp neighbors`

3. **Identifying Misconfigurations:**
   - o Misconfigured network statements or incorrect subnet masks can prevent a routing protocol from properly advertising routes.
   - o **Example:** Check the network statement and ensure that the network address and wildcard mask match the interfaces on which the protocol is supposed to run.

4. **Checking for Routing Loops:**

- o Routing loops can cause traffic to be sent in circles between routers. To troubleshoot this, check for unusual behavior like constant route recalculations or high CPU usage:
  - Use `show ip route` to verify the network paths.
  - Check the router's logs for any messages related to routing issues.

5. **Check for Access Control List (ACL) Issues:**
   - o ACLs can block routing protocol updates. Verify that any ACLs configured on routers are not inadvertently blocking RIP, OSPF, or EIGRP updates. Use `show access-lists` to verify ACL configurations.

6. **Verify Interface Status:**
   - o Ensure that the interfaces involved in routing are up and operational:

```kotlin
Router# show ip interface brief
```

   - If an interface is down, routing updates will not be exchanged.

Summary

In this chapter, you learned how to configure and troubleshoot RIP, OSPF, and EIGRP on Cisco routers. Each protocol offers unique advantages and configurations, with RIP being simple and suitable for small networks, OSPF providing scalability for larger networks, and EIGRP offering faster convergence times and more efficient bandwidth use. Understanding the differences between these protocols and knowing how to configure and troubleshoot them is critical for ensuring reliable and efficient routing in a network.

Part 3

Advanced Networking Concepts

CHAPTER 10

NETWORK ADDRESS TRANSLATION (NAT)

What is NAT and Why is It Used?

Network Address Translation (NAT) is a method used in networking to modify the IP address information in the header of data packets as they pass through a router or firewall. NAT is commonly used to allow multiple devices on a local area network (LAN) to share a single public IP address when accessing the internet.

NAT helps overcome the limitations of the IPv4 address space. Since the number of available IPv4 addresses is finite and running out, NAT allows private networks to use private IP addresses (not routable on the public internet) while still enabling access to the internet through a single public IP address. This helps conserve the public IP address space.

Why is NAT Important?

- **Conserves Public IP Addresses:** NAT allows multiple devices within a private network to share a single public IP address, which helps reduce the consumption of the limited pool of public IPv4 addresses.

- **Enhances Security:** By masking internal IP addresses, NAT helps hide the structure of a private network from external entities, making it more difficult for attackers to target specific devices within the network.

- **Simplifies Network Management:** NAT makes it easier to manage network addresses in large-scale networks since administrators don't have to assign a unique public IP address to each device in a private network.

Types of NAT (Static, Dynamic, PAT)

1. **Static NAT:**

   o **Definition:** Static NAT is a one-to-one mapping between a private IP address and a public IP address. The mapping is fixed and does not change, which makes it suitable for situations where a specific internal device needs to be accessible from outside the network.

   o **How It Works:**

      ▪ A device within a private network (e.g., a web server) is assigned a private IP address, but it is always mapped to the same public IP address for external communication.

      ▪ When external users want to access the web server, they use the public IP address, and NAT translates this to the private IP address of the server.

- o **Example:**
  - Internal Server: 192.168.1.10 → Public IP: 203.0.113.5
  - External users access the server using 203.0.113.5, which is mapped to 192.168.1.10 by the NAT device.

2. **Dynamic NAT:**
   - o **Definition:** Dynamic NAT allows the mapping of private IP addresses to a pool of public IP addresses. The mapping is not fixed and changes dynamically based on availability. When an internal device requests access to the internet, it is dynamically assigned an available public IP from the pool.
   - o **How It Works:**
     - When an internal device makes an outbound request, NAT dynamically assigns it a public IP address from a pool of available public IP addresses. Once the session is completed, the mapping is removed, and the public IP is returned to the pool.
     - **Example:**

- Internal devices: 192.168.1.10, 192.168.1.11
- Available public IP pool: 203.0.113.5, 203.0.113.6
- The device 192.168.1.10 may be assigned 203.0.113.5, and 192.168.1.11 may be assigned 203.0.113.6 for outbound communication.

- **Advantages:**
  - Efficient use of public IP addresses.
  - Each device gets a public IP address when needed, but the mapping is temporary.

3. **Port Address Translation (PAT):**
   - **Definition:** PAT, also known as **NAT overload**, is a type of dynamic NAT that maps multiple private IP addresses to a single public IP address (or a few public IP addresses) by using different port numbers. This allows many devices within a private network to share one public IP address simultaneously.
   - **How It Works:**
     - PAT translates the source IP address and port number for each outbound

connection. When multiple devices on a private network access the internet, PAT assigns unique port numbers to each session, enabling multiple connections to share a single public IP address.

- **Example:**
  - Internal devices: 192.168.1.10, 192.168.1.11
  - Public IP: 203.0.113.5
  - Device 192.168.1.10 connects to a remote server, and NAT assigns it port 1025. Device 192.168.1.11 connects, and NAT assigns it port 1026.
  - The external communication from both devices will appear to originate from 203.0.113.5:1025 and 203.0.113.5:1026 respectively, but both are actually sharing the same public IP.
- o **Advantages:**

- Allows for a large number of internal devices to share a small number of public IP addresses.
- Commonly used in home and enterprise networks to provide internet access to multiple devices using one public IP.

Real-World Applications of NAT

1. **Home Networks:**
   - **Scenario:** In a typical home network, many devices (laptops, smartphones, smart TVs, etc.) need to access the internet. Since IPv4 public IP addresses are limited, NAT allows the router to use one public IP address for all the devices in the household.
   - **How NAT Works:**
     - The router performs NAT and assigns each device in the home a private IP address (e.g., 192.168.1.x). When a device requests internet access, the router translates the private IP address to the public IP address of the router. When data returns from the internet, the router uses PAT to translate the public IP address back to the appropriate private IP address for the requesting device.

2. **Enterprise Networks:**

   o **Scenario:** Large companies with many employees need to provide internet access to hundreds or thousands of internal devices. With NAT, companies can use one or a few public IP addresses and map them to the devices inside their private network.

   o **How NAT Works:**

      ▪ The company's routers perform Dynamic NAT or PAT to map a large number of internal devices to a limited pool of public IP addresses. This reduces the number of public IP addresses needed and ensures that external access to the internet is available for all devices.

3. **Hosting Web Servers:**

   o **Scenario:** A company wants to host a web server within its private network but still needs external users to access it. Static NAT is used to create a one-to-one mapping between the public IP address and the private IP address of the server.

   o **How NAT Works:**

      ▪ External users type in the public IP address assigned to the server (e.g., `203.0.113.5`), which NAT translates to the private IP address of the server (e.g., `192.168.1.10`). This allows the server to be accessible from outside the network while keeping the private network hidden.

4. **Mobile Networks:**

   o **Scenario:** In mobile networks, many mobile devices use private IP addresses assigned by the mobile carrier's internal network. When these devices access the internet, NAT is used to map their private IP addresses to a single public IP address.

   o **How NAT Works:**

      ▪ The mobile carrier's network uses NAT to map the mobile devices' private IP addresses to a single public IP address. This allows the carrier to conserve public IP addresses while still allowing users to access the internet.

5. **Security and Privacy:**

   o **Scenario:** By using NAT, internal IP addresses are hidden from the outside world, providing an added layer of security. It's much harder for external attackers to target individual devices inside a network if their IP addresses are not publicly visible.

   o **How NAT Works:**

- Since NAT masks the internal IP addresses of devices in a private network, it adds a level of obfuscation that makes it more difficult for attackers to directly reach individual devices within the network.

Summary

Network Address Translation (NAT) is a crucial networking technique that allows multiple devices on a private network to share a single public IP address when accessing external resources like the internet. By conserving public IP addresses and enhancing security, NAT has become a fundamental component of modern networking. With different types of NAT—Static, Dynamic, and Port Address Translation (PAT)—network administrators can efficiently manage IP address allocation and ensure secure, seamless communication between internal and external networks. Whether used in home networks, enterprise environments, or hosting public-facing services, NAT plays a vital role in maintaining network efficiency and security.

CHAPTER 11

ACCESS CONTROL LISTS (ACLS)

Introduction to ACLs

Access Control Lists (ACLs) are a set of rules used to filter traffic on a network. ACLs allow network administrators to define conditions for permitting or denying network traffic based on various attributes, such as source IP address, destination IP address, protocol type, port number, etc. ACLs are commonly used to secure network devices, enforce policies, and control the flow of traffic to or from the network.

ACLs are typically configured on routers or firewalls to protect networks, segregate traffic, and prevent unauthorized access to resources. They play a crucial role in defining how and where traffic can flow within a network. ACLs can either permit or deny traffic based on predefined rules.

Types of ACLs:

1. **Standard ACLs:** Used to filter traffic based only on the source IP address.

2. **Extended ACLs:** Used to filter traffic based on more specific parameters, including source and destination IP addresses, port numbers, and protocols.

Configuring Standard and Extended ACLs

1. **Configuring Standard ACLs:**
   o **Definition:** Standard ACLs filter traffic based solely on the **source IP address**. They do not evaluate other aspects of the packet, such as the destination address or protocol type. Standard ACLs are typically used when a simple filter is needed to allow or deny traffic from a specific source.
   o **Syntax:**

   ```
   css
   ```

   ```
   access-list         [ACL-number]
   [permit|deny]  [source  IP  address]
   [wildcard mask]
   ```

   - The ACL-number ranges from 1 to 99 for standard ACLs.
   - The wildcard mask is the inverse of the subnet mask and is used to define the network address range.

103

Example:

- o To permit traffic from a specific network (192.168.1.0/24):

arduino

```
Router(config)#    access-list    10
permit 192.168.1.0 0.0.0.255
```

  - In this example, access-list 10 is the ACL number, permit allows the traffic, and 0.0.0.255 is the wildcard mask, meaning it allows all devices in the 192.168.1.0/24 network.

Step 2: Apply the ACL to an Interface

- o After creating the ACL, you need to apply it to an interface (either inbound or outbound).

arduino

```
Router(config)# interface gigabitEthernet 0/1
Router(config-if)# ip access-group 10 in
```

- o This applies ACL 10 to the inbound traffic on interface gigabitEthernet 0/1.

Example:

- o If you want to deny traffic from the 192.168.2.0/24 network:

  arduino

  ```
  Router(config)# access-list 10 deny
  192.168.2.0 0.0.0.255
  ```

  - This will block all traffic from the 192.168.2.0/24 network while allowing other traffic.

2. **Configuring Extended ACLs:**

   - o **Definition:** Extended ACLs offer more granular control over network traffic. They allow filtering based on both **source and destination IP addresses**, as well as the **protocol type** (e.g., TCP, UDP, ICMP) and specific **port numbers**.
   - o **Syntax:**

     css

     ```
     access-list          [ACL-number]
     [permit|deny] [protocol] [source IP
     address]        [wildcard        mask]
     [destination IP address] [wildcard
     mask] [operator] [port number]
     ```

- The `ACL-number` for extended ACLs ranges from 100 to 199.
- The `protocol` could be TCP, UDP, ICMP, etc.
- The `operator` could be `eq` for equal, `gt` for greater than, or `lt` for less than, used to define port numbers.

Example:

o To allow HTTP traffic (TCP port 80) from the `192.168.1.0/24` network to the `192.168.2.0/24` network:

arduino

```
Router(config)#   access-list   101
permit   tcp   192.168.1.0   0.0.0.255
192.168.2.0 0.0.0.255 eq 80
```

- In this example, the ACL `101` permits TCP traffic from the `192.168.1.0/24` network to the `192.168.2.0/24` network on port 80 (HTTP).

Step 2: Apply the Extended ACL to an Interface

o Similar to standard ACLs, extended ACLs are applied to an interface, either inbound or outbound:

```
arduino
```

```
Router(config)# interface gigabitEthernet
0/1
Router(config-if)# ip access-group 101 in
```

Example:

o To deny all HTTP traffic from the 192.168.1.0/24 network to the 192.168.3.0/24 network:

```
arduino
```

```
Router(config)# access-list 101 deny
tcp      192.168.1.0      0.0.0.255
192.168.3.0 0.0.0.255 eq 80
```

3. **Configuring ACLs on Multiple Interfaces:**

o ACLs can be applied to multiple interfaces to control traffic flowing between different parts of a network. For instance, to block Telnet access to a network from external sources, an extended ACL could be applied to the appropriate interface.

ACL Applications in Network Security

1. **Traffic Filtering:**
   o ACLs are primarily used to filter traffic based on specific parameters. This can include blocking unwanted traffic from external sources, allowing only trusted users to access network resources, or controlling which services are available to users.
   o **Example:** You can create an ACL to allow only specific internal networks to access a web server, while blocking all other incoming traffic from the internet.

2. **Preventing Unauthorized Access:**
   o ACLs can be used to restrict access to certain network segments. For instance, you may want to restrict access to sensitive information by denying access to a specific subnet or allowing only certain users to access a particular resource.
   o **Example:** Use an ACL to block all access from external networks to a critical database server while allowing access from a specific management subnet.

3. **Network Segmentation:**
   o ACLs can also be applied to segment a network into different zones, each with its own access control policies. For example, you can create

different ACLs for each department within a company, limiting the types of communication allowed between departments or between internal and external resources.

o **Example:** ACLs can be used to ensure that the Finance department can only communicate with certain servers and that their traffic is isolated from the rest of the organization.

4. **Securing Remote Access:**

o When remote access is required, ACLs can help restrict which users can connect to the network via VPN or other remote access technologies. Only authorized users or specific IP addresses should be allowed to connect, and ACLs can enforce this restriction.

o **Example:** An ACL can be applied to the router to permit only specific IP addresses (from the company's remote office) to access the corporate VPN, denying any other IP addresses.

5. **Logging and Monitoring:**

o ACLs can be used to log denied or permitted traffic, providing insight into network activity. Logs can be reviewed to track unauthorized attempts to access network resources, which is critical for network security and troubleshooting.

- o **Example:** Using the `log` keyword in an ACL rule can generate logs for any denied traffic. This is useful for monitoring suspicious activity or diagnosing network issues.

```
pgsql

Router(config)# access-list 101 deny
tcp any any eq 23 log
```

6. **Preventing Denial of Service (DoS) Attacks:**
   - o ACLs can help mitigate certain types of DoS attacks by blocking specific traffic patterns or IP addresses that are attempting to overwhelm the network.
   - o **Example:** If a specific IP address is trying to flood the network with traffic, an ACL can be configured to deny traffic from that IP address.

```
arduino

Router(config)# access-list 102 deny
ip 192.168.10.100 0.0.0.255
```

Conclusion

Access Control Lists (ACLs) are a vital component in network security, helping to control the flow of traffic and restrict unauthorized access to network resources. By

110

configuring both **standard** and **extended ACLs**, network administrators can fine-tune network security policies, enforce traffic segmentation, and enhance overall network security. Whether used to filter traffic based on IP addresses, protocols, or ports, ACLs provide essential control over which traffic is allowed or denied access to different parts of a network. Understanding how to configure and apply ACLs effectively is a key skill for anyone managing and securing network infrastructure.

CHAPTER 12

NETWORK SECURITY FUNDAMENTALS

Importance of Network Security

Network security is a critical aspect of any organization's IT infrastructure. It involves measures to protect the integrity, confidentiality, and availability of data and resources as they are transmitted or stored in a network environment. As businesses rely more heavily on digital communication, the need for robust network security becomes even more significant.

1. **Protecting Data and Information:**
   o Sensitive data such as financial records, personal information, intellectual property, and customer data must be safeguarded to prevent unauthorized access or theft. Network security ensures that this data remains private and is only accessible to authorized individuals.

2. **Preventing Unauthorized Access:**
   o Without proper security measures, unauthorized users (hackers, malicious actors, etc.) can infiltrate the network, leading to data breaches, loss of intellectual property, and potential

financial losses. Network security policies and tools such as firewalls, VPNs, and intrusion detection systems are used to prevent unauthorized access.

3. **Ensuring Network Availability:**

   o Cyberattacks, such as Distributed Denial of Service (DDoS), can overwhelm and disable networks, preventing legitimate users from accessing services. Proper security measures ensure that the network is available and operational at all times.

4. **Compliance with Regulations:**

   o Many industries are governed by regulations that require certain levels of network security. For example, healthcare organizations must comply with HIPAA (Health Insurance Portability and Accountability Act) to protect patient information, and financial institutions must comply with PCI-DSS (Payment Card Industry Data Security Standard). Network security helps organizations meet these legal requirements.

5. **Protecting Against Malware and Viruses:**

   o Malware, viruses, and ransomware are significant threats to network security. A compromised device can serve as an entry point for malicious attacks that can spread throughout the network.

Effective security measures help detect, block, and mitigate such threats before they cause harm.

Basics of Firewall and VPN Configurations

1. **Firewalls:**

   o **Definition:** A **firewall** is a network security device or software that monitors and controls incoming and outgoing network traffic based on predetermined security rules. Firewalls are used to create a barrier between a trusted internal network and untrusted external networks, such as the internet.

   o **Types of Firewalls:**

     ▪ **Packet Filtering Firewall:** Inspects each packet of data passing through the network and decides whether to allow or block it based on rules defined by the network administrator.

     ▪ **Stateful Inspection Firewall:** Tracks the state of active connections and makes decisions based on the context of the traffic (i.e., whether the packet is part of an established connection).

114

- **Proxy Firewall:** Acts as an intermediary between internal and external networks, forwarding requests on behalf of the client.

- **Next-Generation Firewall (NGFW):** Includes traditional firewall functions along with advanced features such as intrusion prevention, encrypted traffic inspection, and deep packet inspection.

- **Basic Firewall Configuration on Cisco Devices:**

  - To configure a simple **ACL-based firewall** on a Cisco router:

    ```arduino
    Router(config)#    access-list
    100 permit ip any any
    Router(config)#       interface
    gigabitEthernet 0/1
    Router(config-if)# ip access-
    group 100 in
    ```

  - In this example, traffic is allowed from any source to any destination. More restrictive rules can be applied to block specific types of traffic.

- **Best Practices:**

- Implement a **deny all** rule by default, then selectively allow specific traffic.
- Use **logging** to track and monitor suspicious activity.
- Ensure **high availability** of firewalls by deploying redundant devices.

2. **Virtual Private Network (VPN):**

   o **Definition:** A **VPN** is a secure, encrypted connection that allows remote users or branch offices to access a private network over the internet. It ensures that the data transmitted between the remote device and the internal network is secure and cannot be intercepted.

   o **Types of VPNs:**

      - **Site-to-Site VPN:** Used to connect two networks (e.g., a company's main office to a branch office) over the internet securely.

      - **Remote Access VPN:** Used by individual users to connect to a corporate network from a remote location, such as an employee working from home.

   o **VPN Protocols:**

- **IPSec (Internet Protocol Security):** A suite of protocols that provides secure communication over an IP network by encrypting and authenticating each IP packet.

- **SSL (Secure Sockets Layer):** A protocol commonly used in remote access VPNs for secure communication via a web browser.

o **Basic VPN Configuration on Cisco Routers:**

- For a **site-to-site VPN** using IPSec on a Cisco router:

```arduino
Router(config)# crypto isakmp
policy 10
Router(config-isakmp)#
encryption aes
Router(config-isakmp)#
authentication pre-share
Router(config-isakmp)# group 2
Router(config-isakmp)# exit
Router(config)# crypto ipsec
transform-set myset esp-aes-
256 esp-sha-hmac
```

117

```
Router(config)#    crypto    map
mymap 10 ipsec-isakmp
Router(config)#    set    peer
192.168.1.1
Router(config)# set transform-
set myset
Router(config)#  match  address
100
Router(config)#         interface
gigabitEthernet 0/1
Router(config-if)#  crypto  map
mymap
```

- This sets up a basic IPSec VPN, where
  192.168.1.1 is the IP address of the
  remote peer.

o **Best Practices:**

  - Always use strong encryption and secure
    authentication methods (e.g., certificates,
    pre-shared keys).

  - Monitor VPN connections for unusual
    activity to detect potential security
    threats.

  - Limit VPN access to authorized users
    and resources.

How to Implement Basic Security Measures in a Cisco Network

1. Using ACLs for Traffic Filtering:

- o As discussed earlier, ACLs are an essential tool for controlling traffic. By defining clear rules, ACLs can filter traffic based on source and destination IP addresses, protocols, and port numbers. Implement ACLs to block unauthorized traffic and allow legitimate communication.

Example ACL Configuration:

- o To block Telnet access from external networks but allow it from the internal network:

```arduino
Router(config)# access-list 101 deny
tcp any any eq 23
Router(config)#    access-list    101
permit ip any any
Router(config)#             interface
gigabitEthernet 0/1
Router(config-if)#  ip  access-group
101 in
```

2. Implementing Strong Password Policies:

o Enforce strong password policies on Cisco devices to prevent unauthorized access. Cisco devices allow you to configure different levels of access based on user privileges.

o **Example Configuration:**

arduino

```
Router(config)#    enable    secret
strongpassword123
Router(config)# line vty 0 4
Router(config-line)# login local
Router(config-line)#        password
strongpassword123
```

o The enable secret command configures a strong password for privileged access, and login local forces remote access to use the local user database for authentication.

3. **Encrypting Management Traffic:**

o Use **SSH (Secure Shell)** instead of Telnet to encrypt management traffic between network devices and remote users. SSH ensures that passwords and commands are encrypted, preventing eavesdropping.

o **Example SSH Configuration:**

arduino

```
Router(config)#    ip    domain-name
example.com
Router(config)# crypto key generate
rsa usage-keys label SSH modulus 2048
Router(config)# line vty 0 4
Router(config-line)# transport input
ssh
Router(config-line)# login local
```

4. Network Segmentation with VLANs:

o Implement VLANs to separate different segments of your network. This can help contain security breaches, reduce broadcast traffic, and enhance security by limiting the scope of access between different network segments.

o **Example VLAN Configuration:**

```
arduino

Router(config)# vlan 10
Router(config-vlan)# name HR
Router(config)#            interface
gigabitEthernet 0/1
Router(config-if)# switchport mode
access
Router(config-if)# switchport access
vlan 10
```

5. **Using Intrusion Prevention Systems (IPS):**

   o Implement an Intrusion Prevention System (IPS) to detect and prevent malicious activity in real-time. Cisco's **IPS** is integrated with Cisco routers and can detect known attack signatures, analyze traffic for suspicious patterns, and block potential threats.

6. **Regular Patching and Updates:**

   o Keep all network devices, including routers, firewalls, and switches, up to date with the latest security patches. Cisco regularly releases firmware and security updates to address vulnerabilities in their devices.

7. **VPN for Remote Access:**

   o Set up VPNs for remote workers or branch offices to securely connect to the network. This ensures that sensitive data is protected while in transit across the internet.

Conclusion

Network security is an ongoing process that requires attention to detail and a combination of tools and practices to safeguard against unauthorized access and data breaches. By using firewalls, VPNs, ACLs, and strong authentication measures, Cisco network administrators can implement fundamental security controls to protect network resources. Regularly updating configurations and staying vigilant about emerging threats are key aspects of maintaining a secure network environment.

CHAPTER 13

QUALITY OF SERVICE (QOS)

What is QoS and Why It's Necessary?

Quality of Service (QoS) is a set of technologies and techniques used to manage and prioritize network traffic to ensure that critical applications and services receive the necessary bandwidth and low latency for optimal performance. QoS helps ensure that important traffic—such as voice, video, and mission-critical data—takes precedence over less time-sensitive traffic, such as file transfers or web browsing.

Why QoS is Necessary:

1. **Prioritizing Critical Applications:**
   - o In modern networks, different types of traffic may have different performance requirements. For example, VoIP (Voice over IP) and video conferencing require low latency and high reliability, whereas file transfers and web browsing can tolerate delays. QoS allows network administrators to prioritize latency-sensitive traffic, ensuring that voice and video calls don't experience delays or jitter.

2. **Optimizing Bandwidth:**

   o   With limited network resources, QoS ensures that bandwidth is allocated efficiently. Without QoS, a network can experience congestion, and less critical applications may use more bandwidth than necessary, causing slowdowns for higher-priority applications.

3. **Minimizing Latency and Jitter:**

   o   QoS techniques help reduce **latency** (delay in data transmission) and **jitter** (variations in latency), which are crucial for applications like VoIP, video streaming, and online gaming. A high-quality user experience depends on the ability to minimize these issues.

4. **Managing Network Congestion:**

   o   During periods of high traffic, QoS mechanisms can manage congestion by controlling the rate at which certain types of traffic are transmitted. This ensures that the network remains functional and that critical services are not disrupted by network overloads.

5. **Supporting SLA (Service Level Agreement) Requirements:**

   o   Many businesses have SLAs that require certain services to meet specific performance metrics, such as response time or availability. QoS can help guarantee these metrics by managing traffic flow and ensuring that the performance requirements are met even during times of network congestion.

Configuring QoS on Cisco Devices

1. **Understanding QoS Components:**
   o **Traffic Classification:** Classifies network traffic into categories based on different parameters such as IP address, protocol type, port number, etc.
   o **Traffic Marking:** Marks packets with a specific priority, which helps devices identify how to treat the traffic. Common marking methods include Differentiated Services Code Point (DSCP) and IP Precedence.
   o **Traffic Policing and Shaping:** Defines how much bandwidth is allocated to different types of traffic and how traffic is handled when it exceeds the allocated bandwidth.
   o **Queuing:** Controls how packets are placed in different queues for transmission, ensuring that high-priority traffic is transmitted first.

126

○ **Congestion Management:** Determines how packets are dropped when network resources are unavailable.

2. **Configuring QoS Using Cisco IOS:**

Step 1: Define QoS Policy:

○ Cisco devices use QoS policies to specify how to handle different types of traffic. The policy can be created using **policy maps** and **class maps** to match traffic and define actions (such as prioritizing or dropping traffic).

○ Example: Define a class map to match high-priority traffic (e.g., VoIP):

```arduino
Router(config)# class-map match-any
VoIP
Router(config-cmap)# match ip dscp
ef
```

▪ In this example, the class map VoIP matches traffic with the **EF (Expedited Forwarding)** DSCP value, which is typically used for voice traffic.

Step 2: Create a Policy Map:

127

o   Create a policy map to apply the necessary QoS actions to the matched traffic. For example, prioritize VoIP traffic:

arduino

```
Router(config)#            policy-map
QoS_Policy
Router(config-pmap)# class VoIP
Router(config-pmap-c)# priority 512
```

- In this policy map, the VoIP class is given **priority** treatment, and 512 kbps of bandwidth is reserved for this traffic.

Step 3: Apply the QoS Policy to an Interface:

o   Once the policy map is created, apply it to an interface (either inbound or outbound) to enforce the policy:

arduino

```
Router(config)#            interface
gigabitEthernet 0/1
Router(config-if)#    service-policy
output QoS_Policy
```

- In this example, the `QoS_Policy` is applied to outbound traffic on the `gigabitEthernet 0/1` interface.

3. **Configuring QoS for VoIP:**

   o For VoIP traffic, latency and jitter are critical. Typically, VoIP traffic is classified using the **EF** DSCP value (Expedited Forwarding), and high-priority queuing is used to ensure voice traffic is transmitted with minimal delay.

Example:

arduino

```
Router(config)# class-map match-any VoIP
Router(config-cmap)# match dscp ef
Router(config)# policy-map VoIP_Policy
Router(config-pmap)# class VoIP
Router(config-pmap-c)# priority 128
Router(config)# interface gigabitEthernet
0/1
Router(config-if)# service-policy output
VoIP_Policy
```

   o In this configuration, all traffic with the **EF** DSCP value (indicating VoIP traffic) is classified, and 128 kbps of bandwidth is allocated to ensure priority treatment.

Real-World Scenarios for Implementing QoS

1. **VoIP and Video Conferencing in an Enterprise Network:**

   o **Scenario:** An organization uses VoIP and video conferencing for daily communication. These applications require low latency, low jitter, and minimal packet loss. Without QoS, VoIP and video traffic might compete with other types of traffic like web browsing or file transfers, leading to poor call quality or video lag.

   o **QoS Solution:**

      ▪ Implement **priority queuing** for VoIP and video traffic to ensure that these packets are sent before other lower-priority traffic.

      ▪ Use **DSCP marking** to classify VoIP traffic as high priority, ensuring that voice packets are given precedence over data packets.

      ▪ Apply a **minimum bandwidth guarantee** to ensure that enough bandwidth is allocated to VoIP traffic at all times, even during periods of high network utilization.

2. **Traffic Shaping for Streaming Media:**

   o **Scenario:** A university provides streaming media for online classes. However, the university's network bandwidth is limited, and without QoS, the streaming media might consume too much bandwidth, negatively impacting other critical services like email and cloud-based applications.

   o **QoS Solution:**

     ▪ Use **traffic shaping** to limit the bandwidth for streaming media traffic, ensuring that it doesn't consume excessive bandwidth during peak hours.

     ▪ Implement **traffic policing** to ensure that streaming media traffic conforms to the defined rate limit, dropping packets if necessary to prevent congestion.

3. **Load Balancing for High-Volume Traffic:**

   o **Scenario:** A data center handles high-volume traffic, including web traffic, database queries, and file transfers. Without QoS, all traffic would compete for the same network resources, causing congestion and delays for critical services.

   o **QoS Solution:**

     ▪ Implement **class-based weighted fair queuing (CBWFQ)** to assign different levels of priority to various types of traffic. For example, web traffic and database queries may be given higher priority, while file transfers are treated with lower priority.

- Use **congestion management** to define how to drop traffic during periods of congestion. Less critical traffic (e.g., bulk file transfers) can be dropped, while higher-priority traffic is preserved.

4. **Cloud-Based Applications and Remote Workers:**

   o **Scenario:** Remote workers access cloud-based applications, and network congestion leads to slow application performance, frustrating employees and impacting productivity.

   o **QoS Solution:**

     - Apply **end-to-end QoS** to prioritize traffic between remote workers and cloud applications, ensuring that their traffic receives the necessary bandwidth and low latency.

     - Use **traffic shaping and policing** to prevent remote workers from overwhelming the network with unnecessary traffic, such as large downloads or personal streaming, especially during peak business hours.

5. **Gaming and Online Applications:**

   o **Scenario:** An online gaming service experiences lag or packet loss, affecting gameplay for users. High-priority real-time traffic must be treated with minimal delay to maintain the user experience.

   o **QoS Solution:**

     ▪ Use **priority queuing** for gaming traffic to reduce lag and ensure packets are transmitted in a timely manner.

     ▪ Implement **traffic shaping** to limit less critical traffic during peak hours, ensuring that gaming packets receive the necessary priority.

Summary

Quality of Service (QoS) is essential for managing network traffic effectively and ensuring that critical applications, such as VoIP, video conferencing, and cloud-based services, perform optimally even during times of congestion. By classifying, marking, and prioritizing traffic, network administrators can guarantee that latency-sensitive applications receive the necessary resources and maintain a high level of performance. Configuring QoS on Cisco devices involves using policy maps, class maps, and traffic management techniques such as policing, shaping, and queuing to control how traffic is treated across the network. By implementing QoS in real-world scenarios, organizations can optimize their network performance, enhance user experience, and ensure business-critical services remain available.

CHAPTER 14

WIRELESS NETWORKING

Introduction to Wireless Networks

Wireless networking refers to the use of radio frequency (RF) signals to transmit data between devices without the need for physical cables. Wireless networks enable devices to connect to local area networks (LANs) or the internet without being physically tethered to a network switch or router. Wireless technology has revolutionized the way devices communicate, providing mobility and convenience, particularly in environments where traditional wired connections are not feasible.

Types of Wireless Networks:

1. **WLAN (Wireless Local Area Network):**
   - o WLANs are commonly used in homes, businesses, and public places. They use Wi-Fi (Wireless Fidelity) technology to connect devices like laptops, smartphones, and tablets to a network.
   - o **Wi-Fi Standards:** The most commonly used standards for WLANs are IEEE 802.11a/b/g/n/ac/ax. Each standard defines the

data transmission speeds, frequency bands, and other key features for wireless communication.

2. **WPAN (Wireless Personal Area Network):**

   o WPANs are typically used for short-range communication between devices. Bluetooth is a popular example of a WPAN technology.

3. **WWAN (Wireless Wide Area Network):**

   o WWANs provide wireless coverage over a larger geographical area, such as through cellular networks (3G, 4G, 5G) that offer internet access via mobile devices.

Key Components of a Wireless Network:

- **Wireless Access Point (WAP):** A device that allows wireless devices to connect to a wired network. WAPs typically provide a wireless signal that devices like laptops or smartphones use to communicate with the network.

- **Wireless Router:** A device that combines the functionality of a router and an access point. It connects the local network to the internet, allowing devices to communicate wirelessly.

- **Client Devices:** Devices that connect to the wireless network, including laptops, smartphones, tablets, and printers.

Benefits of Wireless Networking:

- **Mobility:** Users can access the network from anywhere within the coverage area, making wireless networking ideal for dynamic environments such as offices, campuses, or public spaces.
- **Flexibility:** Wireless networks are easier to set up and modify than wired networks, especially in environments where running cables is impractical or costly.
- **Scalability:** Adding more devices or expanding coverage in a wireless network is often simpler than expanding a wired network.

Configuring Basic Wireless Settings in a Cisco Environment

1. **Configuring Wireless LAN (WLAN) Settings on Cisco Devices:**

   Step 1: Enable the Wireless LAN Controller (WLC):

   o Cisco wireless devices typically rely on a **Wireless LAN Controller (WLC)** to manage wireless access points (APs) and wireless network configurations. First, ensure that the WLC is enabled and operational.

```
arduino
```

```
Router> enable
Router# configure terminal
Router(config)# wlan wlan_name wlan_id
Router(config-wlan)# ssid MyWiFiNetwork
Router(config-wlan)# enable
```

- o In this example, the **SSID (Service Set Identifier)** "MyWiFiNetwork" is created, which will be used to identify the wireless network. The `wlan_id` refers to the ID number assigned to the wireless network on the WLC.

Step 2: Configure the Basic Wireless Settings (SSID, Security, and Encryption):

- o Set up the SSID and configure basic security settings, such as WPA (Wi-Fi Protected Access) encryption, to protect wireless communication.

```
arduino
```

```
Router(config)# interface Dot11Radio 0
Router(config-if)# ssid MyWiFiNetwork
Router(config-if)# encryption wlan_name
WPA2
Router(config-if)# authentication open
```

```
Router(config-if)#    key   management   wpa
version 2
Router(config-if)#                passphrase
mySecurePassword123
```

- o This configuration sets up WPA2 encryption and an open authentication method, with a password for network access. It's essential to use strong passwords and WPA2 (or WPA3) encryption to secure the wireless network.

Step 3: Assign IP Addressing and DHCP Settings:

- o Configure the wireless interface on the router to provide IP addresses for devices that connect to the wireless network.

```
scss

Router(config)#       ip     dhcp      pool
MyWirelessPool
Router(dhcp-config)# network 192.168.10.0
255.255.255.0
Router(dhcp-config)#       default-router
192.168.10.1
Router(dhcp-config)# dns-server 8.8.8.8
```

- o In this example, the router is configured to provide DHCP (Dynamic Host Configuration

Protocol) to devices that connect to the wireless network, ensuring they receive appropriate IP addresses.

Step 4: Apply Wireless Settings to Access Points (APs):

o To configure wireless settings on Cisco access points, you can either manually configure each AP or rely on the WLC to push the configuration to all APs in the network.

arduino

```
Router(config)# ap name MyAccessPoint
Router(config-ap)# ssid MyWiFiNetwork
```

o This configuration links the AP to the wireless network you created earlier, allowing it to broadcast the SSID and provide wireless connectivity.

2. **Configuring Advanced Wireless Features:**

o **Band Steering:** Use band steering to optimize wireless performance by directing devices to the 5 GHz band when possible, leaving the 2.4 GHz band for legacy or slower devices.

scss

140

```
Router(config)# dot11 ssid MyWiFiNetwork
Router(config-ssid)# band-steering enabled
```

- o **Channel Selection:** Automatically select wireless channels to minimize interference from neighboring wireless networks.

```
arduino
```

```
Router(config)# interface Dot11Radio 0
Router(config-if)# channel 36
```

Troubleshooting Wireless Networks

1. **Verifying Wireless Connectivity:**
   - o **Check SSID Broadcast:**
     - ▪ If clients cannot see the wireless network, ensure that the SSID is being broadcast. If SSID broadcast is disabled, clients need to manually enter the network name to connect.

```
pgsql
```

```
Router# show wlan summary
```

   - o **Verify Wireless Signal Strength:**

141

- Poor signal strength can cause intermittent connectivity. Use tools like **Cisco Prime Infrastructure** or network analyzers to check signal strength and coverage areas.

pgsql

```
Router# show ap summary
```

2. **Diagnosing Wireless Interference:**

   o Wireless networks can experience interference from other devices (e.g., microwaves, Bluetooth devices) or overlapping channels. Use a tool like **Cisco Wireless Control System (WCS)** or third-party wireless scanners to detect interference and optimize channel selection.

   o **Solution:** Adjust the wireless channel or use **DFS (Dynamic Frequency Selection)** to minimize interference.

3. **Checking DHCP and IP Address Assignment:**

   o If clients are unable to get an IP address or experience network issues, verify that the DHCP server is functioning correctly. Ensure that the router or WLC is correctly assigning IP addresses.

```
arduino
```

```
Router# show ip dhcp bindings
```

- o **Solution:** Check that there are available IP addresses in the DHCP pool and ensure the correct router is acting as the DHCP server.

4. Checking Authentication and Security Settings:

- o Incorrect security settings, such as mismatched WPA keys or authentication methods, can prevent devices from connecting to the network.

```
pgsql
```

```
Router# show wlan security
```

- o **Solution:** Ensure that the correct encryption method (WPA2 or WPA3) and passphrase are configured on both the WLC and the AP.

5. Monitor and Analyze Wireless Clients:

- o Use the command show client on Cisco devices to monitor connected wireless clients, their IP addresses, and the SSID they are connected to.

```
pgsql
```

```
Router# show client summary
```

6. Check Access Point Status:

- o   To troubleshoot AP issues, verify that the AP is operational and communicating with the WLC.

```arduino
Router# show ap status
```

- o   **Solution:** If the AP is not operational, check its physical connection, power supply, and configuration.

Summary

Wireless networking is essential in today's environments, offering flexibility and mobility for users and devices. Configuring wireless networks in Cisco environments involves setting up SSIDs, security protocols, IP addressing, and connecting access points to ensure seamless connectivity. Troubleshooting wireless networks requires tools to monitor signal strength, check DHCP configurations, and ensure correct security settings. By following best practices and leveraging advanced features like band steering and automatic channel selection, network administrators can ensure optimal wireless performance and reliability.

Part 4

Troubleshooting and Maintenance

CHAPTER 15

BASIC TROUBLESHOOTING TOOLS

Using Ping, Traceroute, and Other Diagnostic Tools

1. **Ping:**

   o **Definition:** The **ping** command is one of the most commonly used tools for diagnosing network connectivity. It sends ICMP (Internet Control Message Protocol) Echo Request messages to a target IP address and waits for an Echo Reply. This helps determine if a device is reachable over the network.

   o **How It Works:**

      ▪ When you run a ping command, the system sends packets to the target IP and measures the response time. If the target is reachable, the system responds with the time taken for the round-trip communication. If unreachable, it will time out or provide an error message.

   o **Example Usage:**

   ```python
   ```

   ```
   Router> ping 192.168.1.1
   ```

147

```
PING 192.168.1.1 (192.168.1.1): 56
data bytes
64   bytes   from   192.168.1.1:
icmp_seq=0 ttl=64 time=2.126 ms
```

- o **Common Issues Detected by Ping:**
  - **Packet loss:** If packets are being dropped, this indicates network congestion, poor signal quality, or routing issues.
  - **High latency:** Unusually high round-trip times suggest network delays, possibly due to congestion, routing problems, or distant routing paths.

2. **Traceroute:**

- o **Definition: Traceroute** is a diagnostic tool used to trace the path packets take from one device to another across a network. It identifies each hop between routers on the way to a destination and measures the time it takes to reach each hop.
- o **How It Works:**
  - Traceroute sends a series of packets with incrementing Time-to-Live (TTL) values. Each router that handles the packet decrements the TTL, and when the TTL reaches zero, the router sends back a "time exceeded" message,

allowing the traceroute tool to identify the router's IP and round-trip time.

- o **Example Usage:**

```css
```

```
Router> traceroute 8.8.8.8
Tracing the route to 8.8.8.8
1  192.168.1.1   2 ms   1 ms   1 ms
2  10.0.0.1   4 ms   3 ms   4 ms
3  172.16.0.1   15 ms   12 ms   13 ms
4  8.8.8.8   20 ms   18 ms   19 ms
```

- o **Common Issues Detected by Traceroute:**
  - **Routing loops:** If traceroute shows the same hop repeated in the path, this may indicate a routing loop in the network.
  - **Latency spikes:** If there is a significant delay at a specific hop, it might indicate congestion or hardware issues at that router.

3. **Other Diagnostic Tools:**

- o **Netstat:**
  - **Definition:** The **netstat** command is used to display active network connections, routing tables, and interface statistics. It helps troubleshoot issues

related to open ports, active connections, and overall network statistics.

- **Example Usage:**

```
css
```

```
Router> netstat -an
Active   Internet   connections
(servers and established)
Proto   Recv-Q   Send-Q   Local
Address               Foreign
Address         State
TCP     0         0 0.0.0.0:22
0.0.0.0:*               LISTEN
```

o **NSLookup:**

- **Definition:** The **nslookup** command is used for querying DNS (Domain Name System) servers to resolve domain names into IP addresses.

- **Example Usage:**

```
yaml
```

```
Router>              nslookup
www.example.com
Server:  UnKnown
Address:  192.168.1.1
```

```
Non-authoritative answer:
Name:    www.example.com
Address: 93.184.216.34
```

o **Telnet/SSH:**

  ▪ **Definition: Telnet** and **SSH** are used for remote access to network devices. Telnet is unencrypted, while SSH provides secure communication. These tools are essential for accessing devices like routers, switches, or firewalls for configuration or troubleshooting.

  ▪ **Example Usage (SSH):**

```
css
```

```
Router> ssh admin@192.168.1.1
```

Common Troubleshooting Techniques and Real-World Examples

1. **Checking Physical Layer (Hardware) Connections:**

   o Before diving into network configurations and settings, it's important to check the physical layer. Ensure all cables, routers, switches, and access points are properly connected and powered on.

o **Real-World Example:** A user reports being unable to access the internet. The first step is to check if the router is connected to the modem and if the cable is properly plugged into the port. Sometimes, a loose or faulty cable can be the root cause of connectivity issues.

2. Verify IP Configuration:

o Ensure that devices have valid IP addresses and subnet masks. Misconfigured IP addresses can prevent devices from communicating within the network or accessing the internet.

o **Real-World Example:** A device is unable to communicate with other devices on the local network. Running `ipconfig` (Windows) or `ifconfig` (Linux/macOS) to check the device's IP configuration and comparing it to the network's addressing scheme can reveal misconfigurations or conflicts.

3. Check Routing and Network Path:

o If devices can't communicate across different subnets or networks, check the routing configuration and ensure that routes are correctly defined.

o **Real-World Example:** A remote site can't connect to the main office network. Using **traceroute** can help identify where packets are being dropped, indicating potential routing or firewall issues.

4. **DNS Troubleshooting:**

   o If users can't access websites by name but can access them by IP, DNS resolution might be the issue. Verify DNS settings and perform an `nslookup` to check DNS resolution.

   o **Real-World Example:** Users report being unable to access a website. Running `nslookup` on the domain can show whether the DNS server is resolving the domain correctly.

5. **Check Firewall Settings:**

   o Incorrect firewall rules can block traffic between devices. Ensure that the necessary ports are open for communication and that no rules are inadvertently blocking critical services.

   o **Real-World Example:** A web server is not accessible from the internet. Checking the firewall configuration on both the router and the web server to ensure that port 80 (HTTP) is open is an essential troubleshooting step.

6. **Ping to Local and Remote Devices:**

   o Use **ping** to verify connectivity to local and remote devices. This helps isolate whether the problem lies within the local network or if it's an external connectivity issue.

- o **Real-World Example:** A user cannot reach a remote server. First, ping the local gateway to ensure that the device has network access. Then, ping a remote server to determine if the issue is on the local network or with the external connection.

7. **Check for Network Congestion or High Latency:**
   - o Network congestion or high latency can lead to poor performance. Use tools like **ping** and **traceroute** to check for delays and identify congestion points in the network.
   - o **Real-World Example:** During peak hours, users experience slow internet speeds. Tracing the route to an external server may show a delay at a specific hop, indicating network congestion or an issue with the ISP.

How to Approach Network Issues Systematically

1. **Step 1: Identify the Problem:**
   - o Gather as much information as possible. Ask questions such as:
     - ▪ Are all users affected, or is it limited to one device or location?

154

- Is the issue related to a specific application or service (e.g., web browsing, VoIP, etc.)?
- What error messages or symptoms are occurring?

2. **Step 2: Define the Scope of the Problem:**

   o Narrow down whether the issue is affecting the entire network or only specific devices, subnets, or services. Tools like **ping**, **traceroute**, and **netstat** can help identify if the issue is widespread or isolated.

3. **Step 3: Develop a Hypothesis:**

   o Based on the information you have gathered, come up with a hypothesis regarding the possible causes of the issue. For example, if users can't access a web application, it could be a DNS issue, a firewall configuration, or an application server problem.

4. **Step 4: Test the Hypothesis:**

   o Test your hypothesis by running diagnostic commands or checking configurations. For instance, if you suspect a DNS issue, use `nslookup` or `dig` to verify that the DNS server is functioning correctly.

5. **Step 5: Implement a Solution:**

  o Once the issue is identified, apply the appropriate fix. If it's a misconfigured IP address, correct the settings. If it's a routing problem, update the routing tables accordingly.

6. **Step 6: Verify the Solution:**

  o After applying the fix, verify that the issue is resolved by testing the network functionality. Confirm that affected devices can now connect to the network and services are accessible.

7. **Step 7: Document the Issue and Solution:**

  o For future reference and to help in case the issue reoccurs, document the problem, the steps you took to resolve it, and the final solution. This helps with troubleshooting similar issues in the future and maintains a knowledge base for the network team.

Summary

Basic troubleshooting tools like **ping**, **traceroute**, **netstat**, and **nslookup** are essential for diagnosing network issues. A systematic approach to troubleshooting—starting with identifying the problem, defining its scope, developing hypotheses, testing them, implementing solutions, and verifying results—ensures that network problems are resolved efficiently and effectively. Understanding common network issues, such as connectivity problems, high latency, DNS failures, or firewall misconfigurations, and applying the appropriate diagnostic tools helps ensure a reliable, secure, and well-functioning network.

CHAPTER 16

ADVANCED TROUBLESHOOTING TECHNIQUES

Using Show Commands in Cisco IOS

In Cisco IOS (Internetwork Operating System), **show commands** are essential for gathering information about the status and configuration of network devices. These commands provide detailed insights into the operational state of devices, interfaces, protocols, routing tables, and much more. Understanding how to use these commands effectively is a critical skill for network troubleshooting.

1. **Common Show Commands for Troubleshooting:**
   o **Show Running Configuration:**

   ```lua
   Router# show running-config
   ```

   - This command displays the current configuration of the device. It is essential for understanding the settings, interfaces, and protocols that are actively in use.

   o **Show IP Interface Brief:**

```
kotlin
```

```
Router# show ip interface brief
```

- Provides a quick overview of all interfaces, their IP addresses, and status (up/down). This is particularly useful for checking if an interface is operational.

○ **Show IP Route:**

```
arduino
```

```
Router# show ip route
```

- Displays the device's routing table, showing the paths to different networks and their associated metrics. This command is useful for verifying routing information and diagnosing routing problems.

○ **Show Interfaces:**

```
graphql
```

```
Router#        show        interfaces
gigabitEthernet 0/1
```

- Shows detailed information about a specific interface, including its IP address, traffic statistics, and error counters. It helps diagnose issues related to interface performance, such as packet drops, collisions, or high traffic.

- **Show Version:**

```
pgsql
```

```
Router# show version
```

  - Displays the Cisco device's software version, hardware details, and system uptime. This information is critical for verifying the device's capabilities and ensuring compatibility with various features.

- **Show VLAN Brief:**

```
arduino
```

```
Switch# show vlan brief
```

  - Provides an overview of VLAN configurations, including VLAN IDs and names, and the status of VLANs on a switch.

- **Show Access List:**

```
pgsql

Router# show access-lists
```

- Displays the current access control lists (ACLs) configured on the device. This is helpful for troubleshooting issues related to network traffic filtering.

2. **Using Show Commands to Diagnose Problems:**

   o **Example:** If an interface is down, the `show ip interface brief` command can reveal if there is a physical layer issue, such as a disconnected cable or incorrect configuration. Additionally, `show interfaces` can provide more detailed statistics that help identify the root cause of the problem, such as errors, collisions, or CRC issues.

Debugging Routing and Switching Problems

Debugging tools are used to monitor real-time traffic and events as they occur, providing more granular visibility into network operations. However, debugging can be resource-intensive, so it should be used carefully and typically in a controlled environment.

1. **Using Debug Commands:**

   o **Debug IP Routing:**

   arduino

   ```
   Router# debug ip routing
   ```

   - This command displays detailed information about routing updates and decisions. It's helpful for diagnosing routing table issues or protocol-related problems like RIP, OSPF, or EIGRP.

   o **Debugging OSPF:**

   arduino

   ```
   Router# debug ip ospf events
   ```

   - This command shows detailed information about OSPF (Open Shortest Path First) routing protocol events. It can be used to troubleshoot OSPF neighbor relationships, SPF (Shortest Path First) calculations, and LSAs (Link-State Advertisements).

   o **Debugging EIGRP:**

   arduino

```
Router# debug eigrp packets
```

- Use this to display detailed EIGRP
  (Enhanced Interior Gateway Routing
  Protocol) packet information. This helps
  diagnose issues like routing table
  inconsistencies or slow convergence.

  o **Debugging Switch Port Issues:**

```
arduino
```

```
Switch# debug spanning-tree events
```

- This command helps troubleshoot
  Spanning Tree Protocol (STP) issues,
  including problems with port roles,
  states, or loops.

2. **Best Practices for Debugging:**

   o **Start Small:** Use specific debug commands
   related to the issue at hand. Running broad debug
   commands can overwhelm the device and
   produce excessive output.

   o **Monitor in Real Time:** Use **terminal monitor**
   on remote devices to display debug output in real
   time.

```
arduino
```

```
Router# terminal monitor
```

- o **Disable Debugging After Use:** Always disable debugging once the issue is resolved to avoid performance degradation.

```
arduino
```

```
Router# undebug all
```

3. **Real-World Example:**
   - o **Issue:** A network has been experiencing intermittent connectivity loss between two routers. By using debug ip routing and debug ip ospf events, the network engineer can identify that OSPF is not forming neighbor relationships properly due to mismatched OSPF hello timers, resulting in OSPF failing to converge and dropping routes.

Troubleshooting VLAN, ACL, and NAT Issues

1. **VLAN Troubleshooting:**
   - o **Check VLAN Configuration:**

- Use the `show vlan brief` command to verify that the VLAN exists on the switch and is configured correctly.
- If VLANs are not propagating or devices cannot communicate across VLANs, check trunk links between switches. Trunk ports must allow the relevant VLANs for communication.

```arduino
Switch# show vlan brief
Switch# show interfaces trunk
```

- o **Common Problems:**
  - **Issue:** Devices in different VLANs cannot communicate.
    - **Solution:** Ensure that there is a Layer 3 device (router or Layer 3 switch) with inter-VLAN routing enabled. Verify that the VLAN interfaces are up and properly configured.

2. **ACL Troubleshooting:**
   - o **Verify ACL Configuration:**
     - Use the `show access-lists` command to check the rules in the ACLs.

- **Example:** If a user cannot access a certain service, check the ACL applied to the interface and confirm if the correct rules are in place.

```pgsql
Router# show access-lists
```

- **Common Problems:**
  - **Issue:** An ACL is blocking necessary traffic.
    - **Solution:** Ensure that the ACL is applied in the correct direction (inbound or outbound). Remember that ACLs are evaluated top-down, and the first match is applied. If the ACL is too restrictive, adjust the rules or add exceptions.

3. **NAT Troubleshooting:**
   - **Verify NAT Configuration:**
     - Use the `show ip nat translations` command to check the NAT table and verify if the correct translation rules are applied.

166

```
arduino
```

```
Router# show ip nat translations
```

- **Common Problems:**
  - **Issue:** Internal devices cannot access the internet due to NAT issues.
    - **Solution:** Check if NAT is properly configured on the router and that an **access list** is correctly mapping internal IP addresses to public ones. Ensure that the NAT pool is not exhausted and that the router's interface is correctly mapped for translation.
  - **Use the following command to verify NAT translation settings:**

```
pgsql
```

```
Router# show ip nat statistics
```

4. **Real-World Example:**
   - **VLAN Issue:** Users in the same VLAN but on different switches cannot communicate. After verifying the VLAN configuration, the issue is traced to an incorrect trunk configuration

between the two switches. The trunk port was not allowing the VLAN to pass, preventing the devices from communicating.

o **ACL Issue:** Users are unable to reach the internet. The ACL applied to the router's outbound interface was incorrectly blocking all traffic. After reviewing the ACL configuration, an exception was added for outbound HTTP traffic, resolving the issue.

o **NAT Issue:** External access from internal users was intermittently failing. A review of the NAT configuration revealed that the NAT pool had run out of available IP addresses. After expanding the pool, connectivity was restored.

Summary

Advanced troubleshooting techniques are essential for diagnosing and resolving complex network issues. Using **show commands** in Cisco IOS, such as show ip route, show interfaces, and show vlan brief, provides valuable insights into network performance, routing tables, and device configurations. **Debugging** tools like debug ip routing and debug eigrp packets enable real-time monitoring and provide deeper visibility into network issues.

168

Troubleshooting common network problems, such as **VLAN misconfigurations**, **ACL errors**, and **NAT issues**, requires a methodical approach using the appropriate commands and tools. By following best practices and systematically applying troubleshooting techniques, network administrators can quickly identify and resolve issues to maintain optimal network performance and reliability.

CHAPTER 17

NETWORK MONITORING AND MAINTENANCE

How to Monitor a Network with Tools Like SNMP and NetFlow

1. **Simple Network Management Protocol (SNMP):**

   o **Definition:** SNMP is a protocol used for monitoring and managing network devices, such as routers, switches, firewalls, and servers. SNMP allows network administrators to gather data from devices about performance, traffic, and configuration, as well as to configure devices remotely.

   o **Components:**

      ▪ **Managed Devices:** These are network devices like routers, switches, and servers that can be monitored and managed.

      ▪ **SNMP Agents:** These are software components running on managed devices that collect and store data about the device's performance, status, and configuration.

- **Network Management Systems (NMS):** These are the tools used by administrators to request information from managed devices and present it in a usable format.

- **How It Works:**

  - SNMP uses a **polling** method, where an NMS periodically queries SNMP agents for information. It can also be configured to send **traps** (alerts) when certain events occur.

  - SNMP operates using the **Management Information Base (MIB)**, which is a hierarchical database of network management information.

- **Common SNMP Versions:**

  - **SNMP v1 and v2c:** These are older versions, less secure, and use community strings for authentication.

  - **SNMP v3:** Provides enhanced security with authentication and encryption for data integrity and privacy.

- **Example SNMP Configuration on Cisco Devices:**

  - To enable SNMP on a Cisco device, use the following commands:

171

```
arduino
```

```
Router(config)#              snmp-server
community public RO
Router(config)#              snmp-server
community private RW
```

- This configuration sets the SNMP community string for read-only (RO) and read-write (RW) access. It allows the monitoring of the device's status and allows for device configuration changes through SNMP.

- **Best Practices:**
  - Use **SNMP v3** for enhanced security, as it supports authentication and encryption.
  - Restrict access to SNMP by limiting which devices can query the SNMP agent (via access control lists, or ACLs).
  - Regularly monitor SNMP logs to detect unusual behavior or configuration changes.

2. **NetFlow:**
  - **Definition:** NetFlow is a network protocol developed by Cisco to collect and monitor network traffic data. It provides detailed insights into network traffic patterns,

including the source, destination, and type of traffic. NetFlow helps in identifying network performance bottlenecks, detecting anomalies, and improving network efficiency.

o **How It Works:**

  - NetFlow captures "flows" of data that traverse a device, such as a router or switch. A flow is a sequence of packets with shared attributes like source IP, destination IP, source port, destination port, and protocol.

  - The device then sends this flow data to a **NetFlow collector**, which aggregates and analyzes the traffic data.

o **NetFlow Versions:**

  - **NetFlow v5:** One of the most commonly used versions, provides basic flow records.

  - **NetFlow v9:** A more flexible version that allows customized flow records.

  - **IPFIX (Internet Protocol Flow Information Export):** An open standard version based on NetFlow v9.

o **Example NetFlow Configuration on Cisco Devices:**

- To enable basic NetFlow on a Cisco router:

```
scss


Router(config)# ip flow ingress
Router(config)# ip flow egress
Router(config)#    ip    flow-export
destination 192.168.1.100 9996
```

- This configuration enables NetFlow on incoming and outgoing traffic, and sends flow data to a NetFlow collector at IP 192.168.1.100 on port 9996.

o **Best Practices:**

- Use **NetFlow v9** or **IPFIX** for more detailed and flexible flow records.

- Ensure that NetFlow collectors have adequate processing power to handle the data and provide meaningful analysis.

- Implement flow sampling to reduce the volume of data sent to the NetFlow collector, especially in high-traffic networks.

Best Practices for Network Maintenance

1. **Regular Software and Firmware Updates:**

   o **Why It's Important:** Keeping software and firmware up to date helps patch security vulnerabilities, improve functionality, and maintain network stability.

   o **Best Practice:** Schedule regular updates, ideally during maintenance windows, to minimize disruptions. Always test updates in a lab environment before deploying them in production.

2. **Backup Configurations:**

   o **Why It's Important:** Configuration files are critical for the operation of network devices. If a device fails or is misconfigured, a backup configuration ensures a quick recovery.

   o **Best Practice:** Automate the process of backing up device configurations. Store backups securely and in multiple locations to avoid loss of data.

3. **Network Documentation:**

   o **Why It's Important:** Proper documentation ensures that network devices, configurations, and changes are well-documented, making troubleshooting, upgrades, and repairs easier.

o **Best Practice:** Maintain accurate and up-to-date network diagrams, IP addressing schemes, and configuration change logs.

4. **Monitoring and Alerting:**

   o **Why It's Important:** Continuous monitoring of the network helps detect issues early and ensures the network runs smoothly.

   o **Best Practice:** Use monitoring tools like SNMP, NetFlow, and syslog to gather real-time data on network performance. Configure alerts to notify administrators of critical events (e.g., high CPU utilization, link failures, security breaches).

5. **Traffic Analysis:**

   o **Why It's Important:** Analyzing network traffic helps identify performance issues, bottlenecks, and security threats.

   o **Best Practice:** Regularly analyze traffic data using tools like NetFlow or sFlow to monitor usage patterns and detect unusual behavior that might indicate network issues or attacks.

6. **Network Performance Testing:**

   o **Why It's Important:** Regular performance testing helps ensure that the network meets the required Service Level Agreements (SLAs) and identifies areas for optimization.

- o **Best Practice:** Use tools such as **iperf** or **Wireshark** to test throughput, latency, and packet loss, and compare these metrics against baseline performance.

7. **Security Audits:**

- o **Why It's Important:** Network security is a continuous process, and regular audits help ensure that security policies are being enforced and that the network is protected against new vulnerabilities.

- o **Best Practice:** Schedule regular security audits and vulnerability scans. Ensure that firewalls, ACLs, and intrusion detection/prevention systems (IDS/IPS) are properly configured and regularly updated.

Configuring Cisco Devices for Better Monitoring

1. **Enable SNMP for Monitoring:**

- o **Why It's Important:** SNMP enables network management tools to query Cisco devices for performance and configuration data.

- o **Configuration Example:**

arduino

```
Router(config)#          snmp-server
community public RO
Router(config)#          snmp-server
community private RW
```

2. Enable Syslog for Logging:

- o **Why It's Important:** Syslog is a standard for message logging. It helps keep a log of device events, errors, and status messages, which is essential for troubleshooting.

- o **Configuration Example:**

arduino

```
Router(config)#               logging
192.168.1.100
Router(config)#     logging     trap
informational
```

3. Configure SNMP Traps for Alerts:

- o **Why It's Important:** SNMP traps are alerts that notify network administrators of specific events or issues in real-time.

- o **Configuration Example:**

arduino

```
Router(config)#  snmp-server  enable
traps
```

178

```
Router(config)#   snmp-server   host
192.168.1.100 traps public
```

4. Enable NetFlow for Traffic Analysis:

- o **Why It's Important:** NetFlow allows administrators to collect data about network traffic flows, helping identify bottlenecks or security issues.

- o **Configuration Example:**

```
scss
```

```
Router(config)# ip flow ingress
Router(config)#    ip    flow-export
destination 192.168.1.100 9996
```

5. Configure Interfaces for Monitoring:

- o **Why It's Important:** Monitoring interfaces allows you to track the status, traffic, and errors on network interfaces, providing insights into network health.

- o **Configuration Example:**

```
arduino
```

```
Router(config)#            interface
gigabitEthernet 0/1
Router(config-if)#    ip    address
192.168.1.1 255.255.255.0
```

179

```
Router(config-if)# no shutdown
```

Summary

Network monitoring and maintenance are crucial for ensuring the reliability, performance, and security of a network. Tools like **SNMP** and **NetFlow** provide powerful means for monitoring network traffic, performance, and device health. Cisco devices can be configured for better monitoring by enabling SNMP, syslog, NetFlow, and other diagnostic tools. Best practices for network maintenance include regular updates, backups, documentation, security audits, and continuous performance testing. By following these practices, network administrators can ensure their networks are efficient, secure, and resilient to potential issues.

CHAPTER 18

TROUBLESHOOTING CONNECTIVITY ISSUES

Layer 1 to Layer 3 Troubleshooting

When troubleshooting network connectivity, it's essential to understand the OSI (Open Systems Interconnection) model and its seven layers. Connectivity issues can occur at any layer, and resolving the issue requires systematically working from Layer 1 (Physical) to Layer 3 (Network).

1. **Layer 1 – Physical Layer Troubleshooting:**
   - **Symptoms:** The device is not powered on, cables are not connected, or network interfaces are not operational.
   - **Common Issues:**
     - **Faulty cables:** Physical damage to Ethernet cables or incorrect cable types (e.g., using a crossover cable instead of a straight-through cable) can cause connectivity issues.
     - **Loose or unplugged cables:** Devices may lose connectivity if cables are disconnected or not plugged in securely.

- **Power issues:** A network device (e.g., router, switch) may fail to function if it's not powered on or if it experiences a power failure.
- **Interference:** Electromagnetic interference can cause signal degradation in wired networks, especially in environments with high electrical activity.

Troubleshooting Steps for Layer 1:

o **Check physical connections:** Ensure all cables are properly plugged in, and that devices are powered on.

o **Test cables:** Use a **cable tester** to verify if the Ethernet cables are functioning correctly.

o **Check for link lights:** Most network devices, such as switches and routers, have LEDs indicating the status of interfaces. If the light is off or red, the interface may be down.

o **Inspect for hardware damage:** Visually inspect network ports, cables, and hardware for damage or wear.

o **Try replacing cables or hardware:** If a specific cable or device appears faulty, replace it with a working one to see if connectivity is restored.

2. Layer 2 – Data Link Layer Troubleshooting:

- **Symptoms:** Devices on the same network segment cannot communicate, even though Layer 1 connections appear fine.

- **Common Issues:**

  - **MAC address table issues:** Switches learn and store MAC addresses in a table. If this table becomes full or corrupted, communication can be disrupted.

  - **VLAN misconfigurations:** Devices may be on different VLANs, which can prevent communication even though they are on the same physical switch.

  - **Ethernet frame issues:** Incorrect frame formatting or mismatched duplex settings on switches and devices can cause connectivity problems.

Troubleshooting Steps for Layer 2:

- **Check VLAN configurations:** Ensure that the devices are in the correct VLAN and that the VLAN is properly configured on all switches.

- **Verify switch port configurations:** Ensure ports are in the correct mode (access or trunk) and are assigned to the correct VLAN.

o **Examine the MAC address table:** Use the `show mac address-table` command on Cisco switches to view the learned MAC addresses and verify that they are correct.

o **Check duplex settings:** Mismatched duplex settings (half-duplex vs. full-duplex) on switches and devices can cause communication issues. Use `show interface` to verify duplex settings.

3. **Layer 3 – Network Layer Troubleshooting:**

   o **Symptoms:** Devices can't communicate across different subnets or networks, even though Layer 1 and Layer 2 seem fine.

   o **Common Issues:**

      ▪ **Incorrect IP addressing:** Misconfigured IP addresses, subnet masks, or gateways can prevent devices from communicating with each other across different networks.

      ▪ **Routing issues:** Problems with routing tables or incorrect routing configurations can block traffic from reaching its destination.

      ▪ **Access control lists (ACLs):** ACLs can unintentionally block traffic between networks or between devices.

184

Troubleshooting Steps for Layer 3:

- o **Verify IP configuration:** Use `ipconfig` (Windows) or `ifconfig` (Linux/macOS) to check the IP address, subnet mask, and default gateway on the device.

- o **Ping the gateway:** Verify that the default gateway is reachable. If the gateway is unreachable, check for IP misconfigurations or network segmentation issues.

- o **Check routing table:** Use `show ip route` on routers to verify routing table entries and ensure that routes are correctly configured.

- o **Test connectivity to remote networks:** Use `ping` or `traceroute` to test connectivity to devices in remote networks. If there is no response, the issue might be a routing or ACL problem.

Network Hardware Issues and Resolutions

1. **Switch Issues:**
   - o **Symptoms:** Devices on the same VLAN cannot communicate, or connectivity between switches is unstable.
   - o **Possible Causes:**

- **Port failures:** A faulty port can prevent devices from connecting to the network.
- **Spanning Tree Protocol (STP) loops:** Misconfigurations in STP can cause broadcast storms or network loops, impacting switch performance.
- **MAC address table overflow:** A full or corrupted MAC address table can prevent switches from forwarding traffic correctly.

Resolutions:

- o **Test port connectivity:** If a specific port is causing issues, try connecting a device to another port on the switch or replace the faulty port.
- o **Check for STP issues:** Use `show spanning-tree` to check for loops and verify that STP is properly configured and operational.
- o **Clear the MAC address table:** Clear the MAC address table by using the `clear mac address-table dynamic` command.

2. **Router Issues:**
   - o **Symptoms:** Devices cannot access remote networks or the internet.
   - o **Possible Causes:**

186

- **Routing table issues:** Incorrect or missing routing entries can prevent traffic from reaching its destination.
- **Interface failures:** A downed interface can prevent connectivity, even if the device's routing table is correct.
- **NAT misconfigurations:** Misconfigured NAT (Network Address Translation) settings can block external access to internal devices.

Resolutions:

- **Check the routing table:** Use the `show ip route` command to check if there are proper routes to the destination network.
- **Verify interface status:** Use `show ip interface brief` to verify that interfaces are up and properly configured.
- **Test NAT functionality:** Use `show ip nat translations` to verify that NAT is functioning as expected.

3. **Access Point (AP) Issues:**
   - **Symptoms:** Wireless devices cannot connect to the network or experience intermittent connectivity.
   - **Possible Causes:**

- **SSID issues:** If the SSID is not being broadcasted or mismatched, devices may not be able to join the network.
- **Radio interference:** High interference from nearby devices or physical obstructions can cause wireless connectivity issues.
- **Authentication issues:** Incorrect security settings or mismatched encryption methods can prevent devices from joining the wireless network.

Resolutions:

o **Verify SSID and security settings:** Use `show wlan` to verify the configuration of the wireless network, including SSID and encryption methods.

o **Check signal strength:** Use tools like **Cisco Prime Infrastructure** or **Wi-Fi analyzers** to check signal strength and identify interference.

o **Restart or reset the AP:** Sometimes, restarting the AP can resolve temporary issues caused by resource exhaustion or configuration errors.

Real-World Scenarios for Resolving Connectivity Issues

1. ## Scenario 1: VLAN Misconfiguration

   o **Problem:** Users in different offices, but on the same physical switch, are unable to communicate with each other.

   o **Resolution:** After checking the VLAN configuration, it was discovered that the switch ports were assigned to different VLANs. The solution was to reassign the correct VLANs to the respective ports, and then configure a router or Layer 3 switch to handle inter-VLAN routing.

2. ## Scenario 2: Routing Issues

   o **Problem:** Remote office users cannot access the main office network.

   o **Resolution:** By using `ping` and `traceroute`, it was determined that the routing table on the branch office router did not have a route to the main office. The missing static route was added, and communication between the sites was restored.

3. ## Scenario 3: Access Control List (ACL) Blocking Traffic

   o **Problem:** External users cannot access a web server.

o **Resolution:** An ACL applied to the router was incorrectly blocking HTTP traffic. The `show access-lists` command revealed that an ACL rule was denying access to port 80. The ACL was modified to allow HTTP traffic from external sources, and access was restored.

4. **Scenario 4: Faulty Switch Port**

o **Problem:** A user's device cannot connect to the network, even though the network cable is plugged in.

o **Resolution:** The port on the switch was physically damaged. The user's device was moved to a different port, which resolved the issue. The switch port was also tested with another device to confirm that it was faulty.

Summary

Troubleshooting connectivity issues involves methodically diagnosing problems at each layer of the OSI model, from Layer 1 (Physical) to Layer 3 (Network). By using tools like **ping**, **traceroute**, and **show commands**, network administrators can quickly isolate the cause of the problem. Common issues such as **VLAN misconfigurations, routing table issues, ACL blockages,** and **hardware failures** can be resolved by following a systematic approach and applying the appropriate solutions. By understanding these troubleshooting techniques and real-world scenarios, administrators can efficiently resolve network connectivity issues and ensure reliable network performance.

Part 5

Preparing for the CCNA Exam

CHAPTER 19

EXAM OVERVIEW AND STRUCTURE

The **Cisco Certified Network Associate (CCNA)** exam is a foundational certification for network professionals. It validates the knowledge and skills required to install, configure, and troubleshoot basic networking devices, with a focus on network fundamentals, security, and automation. Here's a guide to understanding the exam format, the key topics to focus on, and how to approach your study for success.

Understanding the CCNA Exam Format

The CCNA exam tests a range of networking topics, from basic networking concepts to more advanced features of IP routing and switching. The format of the exam includes multiple-choice questions (MCQs), drag-and-drop questions, simulations, and performance-based questions.

1. **Exam Code and Duration:**
    o The CCNA exam is designated as **200-301**.

o The exam typically lasts **120 minutes**.

2. **Number of Questions:**

   o The number of questions on the exam can vary, but you can expect approximately **100-120 questions**.

3. **Question Types:**

   o **Multiple Choice Questions (MCQs):** Traditional questions with one correct answer.

   o **Drag-and-Drop Questions:** These involve dragging the correct items to the appropriate positions.

   o **Simulations and Simlet Questions:** These present network scenarios that require you to configure or troubleshoot network devices in a simulated environment.

   o **Performance-Based Questions (PBQs):** In these questions, you are required to perform a task in a real-time, simulated environment, such as configuring a router or troubleshooting a network.

4. **Passing Score:**

   o The passing score for the CCNA exam is typically around **825-850** out of a maximum score of **1000**.

Key Topics to Focus on for the Exam

The CCNA exam covers a broad range of topics in networking, and it's crucial to focus on the key areas that are most likely to appear in the exam. Here's a breakdown of the major topics and subtopics you should prioritize:

1. **Network Fundamentals (20% of Exam):**
   - **OSI and TCP/IP Models:** Understand the OSI and TCP/IP models, including each layer's function and the protocols associated with each.
   - **IP Addressing and Subnetting:** Learn how to assign IP addresses, subnet networks, and perform subnetting calculations. Be familiar with IPv4 and IPv6 addressing schemes.
   - **Network Devices:** Know the roles of routers, switches, hubs, and other networking devices. Understand how each device operates in a network and when to use them.

2. **IP Connectivity (25% of Exam):**
   - **Routing and Switching Concepts:** Understand routing concepts, such as static and dynamic routing, and be able to configure basic routing protocols (RIP, OSPF, EIGRP).

- o **IP Routing:** Learn to configure and troubleshoot routing tables, as well as understand the concept of routing loops and route redistribution.
- o **Switching Concepts:** Be familiar with VLANs, VLAN trunking (802.1Q), and inter-VLAN routing.

3. **IP Services (20% of Exam):**

- o **DHCP:** Know how to configure and troubleshoot DHCP (Dynamic Host Configuration Protocol) for assigning IP addresses dynamically to network devices.
- o **NAT (Network Address Translation):** Understand NAT configurations for translating private IP addresses to public ones.
- o **NTP (Network Time Protocol):** Learn to configure NTP to synchronize the time on network devices.

4. **Security Fundamentals (15% of Exam):**

- o **Access Control Lists (ACLs):** Be familiar with standard and extended ACLs, how they are configured, and their use in filtering traffic.
- o **Security Concepts:** Understand basic security concepts such as network attacks, VPNs, and the importance of network device security (e.g., securing device management access).

5. **Automation and Programmability (10% of Exam):**

- o **Network Automation:** Learn how network devices can be automated using tools like Ansible or Python scripts, and how automation can improve network management and troubleshooting.

- o **SDN (Software-Defined Networking):** Understand the basics of SDN, including its architecture and how it differs from traditional networking.

How to Approach Studying for the CCNA Exam

Studying for the CCNA exam requires a structured and disciplined approach. Below are some effective strategies for preparing for the exam:

1. **Start with the Basics:**

- o Begin by building a strong foundation in networking concepts. Understand the fundamentals of IP addressing, subnetting, and routing. These topics form the basis for more complex network configurations and troubleshooting.

2. **Use Cisco's Official Learning Resources:**

   o   Cisco offers a range of learning materials, including **Cisco Press books, online courses**, and **packet tracer labs**. Use these resources to deepen your understanding of networking concepts and configurations.

   o   **Cisco Networking Academy:** This is an official online learning platform that offers courses specifically designed to prepare students for Cisco certifications like CCNA.

3. **Practice Subnetting:**

   o   Subnetting is a crucial skill for the CCNA exam. Spend time practicing subnetting by hand and using subnetting calculators. Ensure that you are comfortable converting between binary and decimal representations.

   o   Use online tools and apps to test your speed and accuracy in performing subnetting exercises.

4. **Set Up Labs:**

   o   Hands-on practice is essential to understanding networking concepts. Set up your own **CCNA lab** using Cisco Packet Tracer or GNS3. These tools allow you to simulate real-world networking scenarios and practice configuring routers, switches, and network protocols.

- o **Simulated exams** or practice exams are also useful to get a feel for the types of questions that may appear on the real exam.

5. **Focus on Troubleshooting:**
   - o The CCNA exam includes performance-based questions (PBQs) that require you to troubleshoot and configure network devices. Make sure to practice troubleshooting network configurations and diagnose problems in lab scenarios.
   - o Pay special attention to common network issues like IP addressing conflicts, VLAN misconfigurations, and routing issues.

6. **Use Study Guides and Practice Exams:**
   - o Study guides and practice exams are valuable tools for gauging your understanding of key topics. They help identify areas where you may need further study and can improve your time management for the exam.
   - o Try to take **practice exams** under timed conditions to simulate the pressure of the real exam.

7. **Join Study Groups:**
   - o Joining a study group or participating in online forums such as Reddit, Cisco Learning Network, or other networking communities can provide

support, answer questions, and share valuable insights.

8. Allocate Time for Revision:

o   As the exam date approaches, allocate time to review the topics you find most challenging. Focus on weak areas and review key configuration examples, commands, and troubleshooting steps.

9. Don't Cram:

o   Avoid cramming all the material at once. Consistent study over weeks or months is more effective than attempting to absorb all the material in a short time period. Take regular breaks and ensure you're getting enough rest.

10. Stay Positive and Confident:

o   The CCNA exam can be challenging, but with the right preparation, you can succeed. Stay positive, manage your study time effectively, and don't be afraid to ask for help when needed.

Summary

The **CCNA exam** is a comprehensive test that assesses your knowledge and skills in network configuration, management, and troubleshooting. To prepare for the exam, focus on mastering key topics such as IP addressing, routing, VLANs, network security, and automation. Use a combination of study materials, hands-on labs, practice exams, and troubleshooting exercises to ensure you understand the core concepts and can apply them in real-world scenarios. By approaching your study systematically and dedicating time to practice, you'll be well on your way to passing the CCNA exam and taking your first step towards becoming a certified network professional.

You said:

19. Cisco IOS Command-Line Interface (CLI) o Importance of Cisco CLI for CCNA o Common Cisco commands explained with examples o Configuring devices using CLI

ChatGPT said:

Chapter 19: Cisco IOS Command-Line Interface (CLI)

Importance of Cisco CLI for CCNA

The **Cisco IOS Command-Line Interface (CLI)** is a powerful tool used for configuring and managing Cisco devices such as routers, switches, and firewalls. For CCNA certification, having a strong grasp of the Cisco CLI is essential. The CLI allows network administrators to access and configure Cisco devices, monitor network status, troubleshoot, and secure network infrastructure effectively.

1. **Why CLI is Crucial for CCNA:**
   o **Essential Configuration Tool:** Nearly all configurations for Cisco devices are done through the CLI, making it the primary method of interacting with the device.
   o **Efficient Troubleshooting:** The CLI provides access to real-time diagnostics, making it invaluable for troubleshooting network problems. By using show commands, network administrators can check device status, routing tables, interfaces, and configurations.
   o **Required for Exam:** The CCNA exam will require you to perform device configuration tasks using the CLI. Understanding how to enter and exit configuration modes, and knowing which commands are used for specific configurations, is critical for passing the exam.

2. **Learning the CLI Syntax:**
   o Cisco CLI follows a straightforward structure, where you enter commands in different modes (user mode, privileged exec mode, and global configuration mode) to perform various tasks.

o **User Mode:** Allows basic commands like checking device status.

o **Privileged Exec Mode:** Provides access to more advanced commands and settings, such as configuration and monitoring tools.

o **Global Configuration Mode:** Enables you to configure various aspects of the device, including IP settings, routing protocols, and interface configurations.

Common Cisco Commands Explained with Examples

Here are some of the most commonly used Cisco CLI commands, along with examples to help you understand how to use them:

1. **Basic Navigation Commands:**

   o **Enable (Enter Privileged Mode):**

   ```shell
   Router> enable
   Router#
   ```

   - This command allows access to privileged exec mode, where most configuration and troubleshooting commands are available.

- o **Exit (Exit from CLI Mode):**

```shell
Router# exit
Router>
```

  - The `exit` command takes you back to the previous mode or logs you out of the device.

2. **Show Commands (Monitoring and Diagnostics):**
   - o **Show Running Configuration:**

```lua
Router# show running-config
```

     - Displays the device's active configuration. This is useful for reviewing changes, verifying current settings, and troubleshooting.
   - o **Show IP Interface Brief:**

```kotlin
Router# show ip interface brief
```

- Provides a summary of the device's interfaces, including their status (up/down), IP addresses, and any administrative issues.

- o **Show Version:**

```pgsql
Router# show version
```

- Displays information about the router's software version, system uptime, and hardware details.

- o **Show IP Route:**

```arduino
Router# show ip route
```

- Displays the routing table, which contains the best paths to reach different networks. This is crucial for troubleshooting routing issues.

3. **Configuration Commands:**

- o **Enter Global Configuration Mode:**

```arduino
```

```
Router# configure terminal
Router(config)#
```

- This command allows you to enter configuration mode, where you can modify the device's settings.

o **Set Hostname:**

```
scss
```

```
Router(config)# hostname Router1
Router1(config)#
```

- Configures the device's hostname. This is useful for identifying devices in a network.

o **Assign IP Address to an Interface:**

```
arduino
```

```
Router1(config)#          interface
gigabitEthernet 0/1
Router1(config-if)#    ip    address
192.168.1.1 255.255.255.0
Router1(config-if)# no shutdown
```

- This command assigns an IP address and subnet mask to an interface. The no shutdown command ensures that the interface is enabled.

- **Enable Interface:**

arduino

```
Router1(config-if)# no shutdown
```

- This command enables an interface that has been administratively shut down (i.e., disabled).

4. Routing Configuration Commands:

- **Configure Static Routing:**

arduino

```
Router1(config)#      ip      route
192.168.2.0           255.255.255.0
192.168.1.2
```

- This command configures a static route, telling the router how to reach a destination network (in this case, 192.168.2.0/24) through the next hop (192.168.1.2).

- **Configure Routing Protocol (RIP):**

arduino

```
Router1(config)# router rip
Router1(config-router)#      network
192.168.1.0
Router1(config-router)#      network
192.168.2.0
```

- This example configures RIP as the routing protocol and advertises networks for RIP to use.

5. **Security Configuration Commands:**

   o **Configure Password for Privileged Exec Mode:**

   ```
   arduino
   ```

   ```
   Router1(config)#    enable    secret
   mySecurePassword
   ```

   - Configures a secure password for accessing privileged exec mode.

   o **Configure Console Password:**

   ```
   arduino
   ```

   ```
   Router1(config)# line con 0
   Router1(config-line)#      password
   myConsolePassword
   Router1(config-line)# login
   ```

- Configures a password for accessing the device via the console.

○ **Configure SSH for Remote Access:**

arduino

```
Router1(config)#    ip    domain-name
example.com
Router1(config)# crypto key generate
rsa usage-keys label SSH modulus 2048
Router1(config)# line vty 0 4
Router1(config-line)#        transport
input ssh
Router1(config-line)# login local
```

- This sets up SSH (secure shell) for secure remote access to the router.

6. Saving Configuration:

○ **Save Running Configuration to Startup Configuration:**

lua

```
Router1#    running-config    startup-
config
```

- This command saves the current configuration to memory, ensuring that the settings persist after a reboot.

209

Configuring Devices Using CLI

To configure Cisco devices effectively, follow these steps:

1. **Access the Device:**
   - Connect to the router, switch, or firewall using a console cable or over the network via SSH or Telnet.
   - Once connected, you will be in **user mode** (Router>).

2. **Enter Privileged Exec Mode:**
   - From user mode, type the `enable` command to enter privileged exec mode (Router#).

3. **Enter Global Configuration Mode:**
   - From privileged exec mode, type `configure terminal` to enter global configuration mode (Router(config)#), where you can make changes to the device configuration.

4. **Configure Interfaces and Routing:**
   - Assign IP addresses to interfaces, configure routing protocols, and apply security settings. For example:

   ```
   arduino
   ```

```
Router(config)#           interface
gigabitEthernet 0/1
Router(config-if)#   ip   address
192.168.1.1 255.255.255.0
Router(config-if)# no shutdown
```

5. **Verify Configuration:**

   o Use commands like `show ip interface brief`, `show running-config`, and `show ip route` to verify that your changes are applied correctly and that the device is functioning as expected.

6. **Save Your Configuration:**

   o After configuring the device, save the running configuration to ensure that changes are not lost after a reboot:

   ```lua
   Router#      running-config  startup-config
   ```

Summary

The **Cisco IOS CLI** is a crucial tool for managing Cisco devices. As part of CCNA preparation, mastering the Cisco CLI is essential for configuring routers and switches, troubleshooting network issues, and implementing network protocols. By learning common commands and their syntax—such as configuring IP addresses, routing protocols, security settings, and verifying configurations—you can efficiently manage network devices. Hands-on practice with the CLI will build your confidence in device configuration and troubleshooting, which is key to passing the CCNA exam.

CHAPTER 20

LAB EXERCISES AND PRACTICAL EXAMPLES

Hands-On Lab Exercises for Each Key Concept

One of the best ways to prepare for the **CCNA exam** is through hands-on lab exercises that simulate real-world scenarios. These exercises help solidify your understanding of networking concepts and give you the practical experience needed to troubleshoot and configure networks efficiently. Below are lab exercises for some key CCNA concepts.

---

1. Basic IP Addressing and Subnetting Lab

Objective: Learn how to assign IP addresses, create subnets, and verify configurations.

Lab Steps:

1. **Create Subnets:**

    o Given the network `192.168.1.0/24`, divide it into four subnets. What are the subnet masks, and what are the first three subnets?

213

- o **Subnet 1:** 192.168.1.0/26
- o **Subnet 2:** 192.168.1.64/26
- o **Subnet 3:** 192.168.1.128/26
- o **Subnet 4:** 192.168.1.192/26

2. **Assign IP Addresses to Devices:**
   - o Assign the following IP addresses:
     - Router 1: 192.168.1.1/26
     - Router 2: 192.168.1.65/26
     - Host 1: 192.168.1.2/26
     - Host 2: 192.168.1.66/26

3. **Verify Subnetting:**
   - o Use show ip interface brief on both routers and ipconfig on hosts to verify IP configurations.
   - o Ping between devices to test connectivity.

---

2. Configuring VLANs on a Cisco Switch

Objective: Learn how to configure and assign VLANs on a Cisco switch.

Lab Steps:

1. **Create VLANs:**

    o   Create VLAN 10 for the Sales team and VLAN 20 for the Marketing team.

arduino

```
Switch(config)# vlan 10
Switch(config-vlan)# name Sales
Switch(config)# vlan 20
Switch(config-vlan)# name Marketing
```

2. **Assign VLANs to Switch Ports:**

    o   Assign ports 1-10 to VLAN 10 and ports 11-20 to VLAN 20.

arduino

```
Switch(config)#       interface       range
fastEthernet 0/1 - 10
Switch(config-if-range)#  switchport  mode
access
Switch(config-if-range)# switchport access
vlan 10

Switch(config)#       interface       range
fastEthernet 0/11 - 20
Switch(config-if-range)#  switchport  mode
access
Switch(config-if-range)# switchport access
vlan 20
```

3. Verify VLANs and Port Assignments:

- o Use `show vlan brief` to verify the VLAN configurations and port assignments.
- o Test connectivity between hosts in the same VLAN and ensure that devices in different VLANs cannot communicate without a router or Layer 3 switch.

---

3. Configuring Static Routing

Objective: Learn how to configure static routing between two routers.

Lab Steps:

1. Set Up Two Routers:

- o Router 1: Interface 1: `192.168.1.1/24`
- o Router 2: Interface 2: `192.168.2.1/24`

2. Configure Static Routing:

- o On Router 1, add a static route to reach the `192.168.2.0/24` network through Router 2.

```
arduino
```

```
Router1(config)#  ip  route  192.168.2.0
255.255.255.0 192.168.1.2
```

o On Router 2, add a static route to reach the 192.168.1.0/24 network through Router 1.

arduino

```
Router2(config)#   ip   route   192.168.1.0
255.255.255.0 192.168.2.2
```

3. **Verify the Static Routes:**

   o Use show ip route on both routers to verify the static routes.

   o Test connectivity between devices in different networks by pinging 192.168.2.1 from a host in 192.168.1.0/24 and vice versa.

4. Configuring NAT (Network Address Translation)

Objective: Learn how to configure NAT for Internet access.

Lab Steps:

1. **Set Up a Router for NAT:**

   o Configure Router 1 with the following network interfaces:

     - Inside network: 192.168.1.0/24

     - Outside network: 203.0.113.1 (public IP address)

2. Configure NAT:

o Configure NAT overload (PAT) to allow multiple devices in the private network to share a single public IP.

scss

```
Router1(config)#  access-list  1  permit
192.168.1.0 0.0.0.255
Router1(config)# ip nat inside source list
1 interface Ethernet0 overload
```

3. Configure Interface Settings:

o Define the inside and outside interfaces:

scss

```
Router1(config)# interface Ethernet0
Router1(config-if)# ip nat outside

Router1(config)# interface Serial0
Router1(config-if)# ip nat inside
```

4. Test NAT:

o Use show ip nat translations to verify that NAT translations are happening correctly.

- o Test Internet access from a host in the `192.168.1.0/24` network by pinging an external IP.

---

5. Configuring Access Control Lists (ACLs)

Objective: Learn how to configure standard and extended ACLs for traffic filtering.

Lab Steps:

1. **Create a Standard ACL:**
   - o Block access to `192.168.2.0/24` from the `192.168.1.0/24` network.

   arduino

   ```
   Router1(config)#   access-list   10   deny
   192.168.2.0 0.0.0.255
   Router1(config)# access-list 10 permit any
   ```

2. **Apply ACL to an Interface:**
   - o Apply the ACL to the inbound interface to restrict traffic.

   arduino

```
Router1(config)# interface Ethernet0
Router1(config-if)# ip access-group 10 in
```

3. Verify ACL:

- o Use `show access-lists` to view the configured ACL.
- o Test the connectivity from `192.168.1.0/24` to `192.168.2.0/24` and verify that traffic is blocked.

Configuring Devices in a Simulated Environment

Objective: Set up a network in a simulated environment using Cisco Packet Tracer, GNS3, or similar tools.

Lab Steps:

1. Set Up a Basic Network:

- o Create a simple network with two routers, two switches, and four hosts.
- o Assign IP addresses and configure routing between the routers.

2. Simulate Communication:

- o Test connectivity using `ping` between devices in different parts of the network.

- o Configure additional services like DHCP, NAT, and VLANs to make the network functional.

3. **Monitor and Troubleshoot:**
   - o Use tools like **Packet Tracer** or **Wireshark** to capture and analyze packets.
   - o Troubleshoot connectivity issues by using CLI commands like `ping`, `show ip route`, and `show interfaces`.

Practice Problems to Test Your Knowledge

1. **IP Addressing and Subnetting:**
   - o Given a network `172.16.0.0/22`, how many subnets can you create, and what will be the subnet mask for each subnet? Assign IP addresses to the first three subnets.

2. **VLAN Configuration:**
   - o You have two VLANs: VLAN 10 (Sales) and VLAN 20 (Marketing). How would you configure these VLANs on a Cisco switch, and how would you assign ports 1-10 to VLAN 10 and ports 11-20 to VLAN 20?

3. **Static Routing:**
   - o Configure static routes to allow communication between the `192.168.10.0/24` and

`192.168.20.0/24` networks through a router with IP addresses `192.168.1.1` and `192.168.2.1` on two different interfaces.

4. **ACL Configuration:**

   o Write an ACL that permits access from the `192.168.1.0/24` network to the `192.168.2.0/24` network but denies access from `192.168.3.0/24`.

5. **Network Troubleshooting:**

   o Given a topology with multiple routers, switches, and hosts, identify the root cause of a connectivity issue. Use tools like `ping`, `traceroute`, and `show commands` to diagnose the problem and resolve it.

Summary

Lab exercises and practical examples are essential in mastering the concepts required for the CCNA exam. By configuring real-world scenarios such as IP addressing, VLANs, static routing, NAT, and ACLs, you gain hands-on experience that deepens your understanding of networking concepts. Simulating these configurations in tools like Cisco Packet Tracer or GNS3 allows you to experiment with network setups and troubleshoot issues, which is vital for both the exam and real-world network management. Practice problems test your knowledge and help you develop the confidence needed to succeed in the CCNA exam.

CHAPTER 21

NETWORK DESIGN BEST PRACTICES

Real-World Network Design Scenarios

Effective network design is crucial for creating networks that are efficient, secure, and scalable. Below are a few real-world network design scenarios that demonstrate different design principles and considerations:

1. **Small Business Network Design:**
   - **Scenario:** A small business with 50 employees requires a simple, secure, and cost-effective network. The network must support VoIP phones, basic data transfer, email, and web browsing. The business needs minimal redundancy but should have a secure perimeter and manageable growth capabilities.
   - **Design Considerations:**
     - **Topological Choice:** A **star topology** is ideal for small networks, with a central switch connecting all end devices and servers.
     - **Subnetting:** The network will be subnetted to segregate different services

(e.g., administrative systems, employee devices, guest network).

- **Firewall and Security:** A **firewall** is placed at the network edge to protect against external threats. Additionally, access control lists (ACLs) are implemented to limit internal access between subnets.

- **Reliability:** A **single internet connection** with a failover link to a mobile hotspot or second ISP can ensure continuity of service in case of a primary ISP failure.

- **Future Growth:** Allow room for growth by providing extra ports on the switch and ensuring that the router can handle more devices and traffic as the business scales.

2. **Large Enterprise Network Design:**

   o **Scenario:** A large enterprise with multiple departments, hundreds of employees, and several remote offices requires a robust, secure, and high-performance network. The network needs to support real-time applications like VoIP and video conferencing, as well as provide remote access to employees.

o **Design Considerations:**

- **Hierarchical Network Design:** The **three-tier architecture** (core, distribution, and access layers) is used for scalability, performance, and redundancy.

- **Core Layer:** High-performance core switches connect the data centers, facilitating fast, low-latency data transfers.

- **Distribution Layer:** Distribution switches handle routing, quality of service (QoS) management, and VLANs, ensuring efficient traffic management.

- **Access Layer:** Access switches connect end devices to the network and provide Power over Ethernet (PoE) to VoIP phones and other devices.

- **Redundancy and Fault Tolerance:** Implement **HSRP (Hot Standby Router Protocol)** or **VRRP (Virtual Router Redundancy Protocol)** at the core layer to ensure router redundancy. Use **EtherChannel** for link aggregation between switches to increase bandwidth and provide failover.

226

- **Remote Access:** Use a **VPN (Virtual Private Network)** or direct access solutions like **SD-WAN** to provide secure, encrypted connections for remote employees.

3. **Data Center Network Design:**
   - **Scenario:** A company is designing a data center network to handle cloud computing services, storage, and enterprise applications. The network needs to be highly available, with minimal downtime, and capable of scaling to meet increasing demand.
   - **Design Considerations:**
     - **Spine-Leaf Architecture:** A **spine-leaf topology** is used to provide high bandwidth, low latency, and scalability. Each leaf switch is connected to every spine switch, ensuring that traffic between any two devices can be routed through the least congested path.
     - **Redundancy:** Use redundant power supplies, links, and paths to ensure that there is no single point of failure. **Dual-homed connections** to the core and edge switches provide additional fault tolerance.

- **Load Balancing:** Implement **software-defined networking (SDN)** for load balancing and dynamic traffic management across servers and applications.
- **Storage Network:** A **dedicated storage area network (SAN)** or **network-attached storage (NAS)** is integrated into the network for high-performance, scalable data storage.

Best Practices for Designing Reliable and Scalable Networks

Designing a network that is both reliable and scalable is critical to ensuring long-term performance and growth. Here are some best practices to follow when designing such a network:

1. **Understand the Business Requirements:**
   o Always begin with a clear understanding of the business needs and objectives. A network should support the business's goals, whether it's for enabling digital transformation, supporting remote employees, or improving customer services. Aligning network design with business

goals ensures that the infrastructure is designed appropriately.

2. **Scalable Design:**

   o **Modular Design:** Design the network in modules that can be easily scaled as the business grows. This approach allows for the addition of devices, users, and services without a complete redesign. Modular components can include routers, switches, firewalls, and wireless access points.

   o **Bandwidth Planning:** Calculate the required bandwidth for each segment of the network and ensure that there is sufficient capacity for growth. Always design with future bandwidth requirements in mind to avoid congestion as the number of users or devices increases.

   o **Virtualization:** Consider network **virtualization** (e.g., VLANs, VRFs) to separate traffic and provide scalable solutions for different departments or applications.

3. **Redundancy and Fault Tolerance:**

   o **Dual-Path Networks:** Use dual-path connections and failover mechanisms to provide fault tolerance. For instance, use two or more physical connections between critical devices and utilize protocols like **Spanning Tree Protocol**

(STP) and **EtherChannel** to eliminate single points of failure.

o **Load Balancing:** Implement load balancing to distribute traffic efficiently across the network, preventing congestion and improving overall network performance. Techniques such as **DNS load balancing**, **link aggregation**, and **software-defined networking (SDN)** can be useful in balancing traffic across multiple paths.

o **UPS (Uninterruptible Power Supply):** Ensure that critical network devices, such as routers and switches, have backup power to maintain network operations during power outages.

4. **Security:**

o **Network Segmentation:** Use VLANs and subnetting to isolate traffic between different network segments. For instance, separate guest and employee networks to enhance security and reduce the impact of any security breaches.

o **Access Control Lists (ACLs):** Use ACLs to control which devices and users can access specific resources. Configure ACLs on routers and firewalls to protect sensitive data and prevent unauthorized access.

o **Firewalls and IDS/IPS:** Deploy firewalls and Intrusion Detection/Prevention Systems

(IDS/IPS) at critical points in the network to monitor and block malicious traffic.

- o **Network Access Control (NAC):** Use NAC systems to ensure that devices connecting to the network are compliant with security policies.

5. **Centralized and Distributed Management:**

- o **Centralized Management Tools:** Use network management platforms (e.g., **Cisco Prime, SolarWinds**), to monitor and manage network performance, configurations, and troubleshooting. Centralized management tools provide a unified view of the entire network, making it easier to identify and address issues quickly.

- o **Distributed Control:** For larger networks, use distributed management techniques to delegate responsibilities for network monitoring, security, and traffic management. This ensures the network can scale while maintaining efficient oversight.

How to Ensure Network Resilience and Fault Tolerance

1. **Design for High Availability:**

- o **Redundant Paths:** Ensure that multiple physical and logical paths are available between critical network devices. This includes **dual links** between switches, routers, and firewalls to ensure no single path failure disrupts the network.

- o **Automatic Failover:** Implement protocols like **HSRP** or **VRRP** to allow for automatic failover between routers. This ensures that if one router fails, another router will take over without impacting the network.

- o **Link Aggregation:** Combine multiple network interfaces using **EtherChannel** or similar technologies to increase the bandwidth and provide automatic failover in case of a link failure.

2. **Monitor Network Health:**

- o **Proactive Monitoring:** Implement proactive network monitoring to detect potential problems before they cause network outages. Use SNMP, NetFlow, or syslog to continuously monitor devices for performance, security breaches, and configuration changes.

- o **Real-time Alerts:** Set up alerting mechanisms to notify administrators of any network disruptions, interface failures, or security incidents.

3. **Disaster Recovery and Backup:**

- o **Backup Configurations:** Regularly backup device configurations and network diagrams to

232

facilitate a fast recovery in case of network failure.

- o **Disaster Recovery Plan:** Develop a comprehensive disaster recovery plan that includes steps for restoring services, rerouting traffic, and recovering data after a catastrophic failure.

4. **Test Resilience Regularly:**

- o **Failover Testing:** Periodically test network failover scenarios to ensure that redundancy and failover mechanisms work as expected. This includes simulating router or link failures and verifying that traffic reroutes as intended.

- o **Load Testing:** Simulate heavy traffic conditions to ensure that the network can handle peak loads without failure or significant degradation in performance.

Summary

Designing reliable, scalable, and resilient networks is key to ensuring business continuity, performance, and security. By following best practices such as modular design, redundancy, and security measures, network administrators can create infrastructures that meet both current needs and future growth. A focus on fault tolerance, high availability, and network resilience ensures that the network can handle unexpected failures without significant downtime. Regular monitoring, testing, and proactive management are crucial for maintaining a healthy network environment and ensuring optimal performance.

CHAPTER 22

TIME MANAGEMENT AND EXAM STRATEGY

Tips for Managing Time During the Exam

Managing your time efficiently during the **CCNA exam** is crucial to ensure that you complete all sections and have sufficient time to review your answers. Here are some strategies to help you manage your time during the exam:

1. **Understand the Exam Structure:**
   o The CCNA exam consists of multiple-choice questions, simulations, and performance-based questions. Typically, you'll have 100-120 questions to complete in 120 minutes. This gives you roughly **1 to 1.5 minutes per question**.
   o **Tip:** Familiarize yourself with the structure of the exam beforehand so you can allocate time for each section appropriately.

2. **Start with the Simulations:**
   o **Why:** Simulations often take longer to complete because they require you to configure devices, troubleshoot networks, or analyze network behavior. By tackling them early when your mind

is fresh, you reduce the risk of running out of time.

- o **Tip:** Allocate 20-25 minutes for the simulations at the beginning of the exam.

3. **Set Time Limits for Each Section:**

- o **Multiple Choice Questions (MCQs):** Aim to spend around **1 minute per question** on MCQs. If you're unsure about an answer, mark it for review and come back to it later. This prevents you from getting stuck on a difficult question.

- o **Simulations:** Spend **20-25 minutes** on each simulation. If you complete it early, use the extra time to double-check your work.

- o **Review Time:** Reserve at least **10-15 minutes** at the end of the exam to review your answers. If you're unsure about any question, make a final review.

4. **Pace Yourself:**

- o If you find yourself spending too much time on a single question or section, move on to the next. It's better to skip a difficult question and come back to it later than to waste valuable time.

- o **Tip:** Use the **flag for review** feature. Mark questions that need more time and return to them after completing the other sections.

5. **Manage Stress:**

- o Take a deep breath if you start feeling rushed or stressed. Stress can cloud your judgment and slow you down. Keeping calm and focused will help you think clearly and maintain your pace throughout the exam.

How to Prioritize Questions and Avoid Common Pitfalls

1. **Prioritize Easy Questions First:**
   - o Start by answering the questions you are most confident about. This helps build momentum and ensures you're accumulating points quickly.
   - o **Tip:** If you encounter a question that feels too challenging or time-consuming, mark it for later and move on to the next one. Coming back to it with a clear mind may help you recall the answer.

2. **Don't Spend Too Much Time on One Question:**
   - o If a question is taking longer than expected and you're not sure of the answer, skip it and come back later. Spending too much time on one question can hurt your overall performance, especially in an exam with a time limit.
   - o **Tip:** The rule of thumb is to spend no more than **2 minutes** on a question if you're unsure. If you still don't know the answer, guess based on your knowledge and mark it for review.

3. Avoid Second-Guessing Yourself:

- o Often, your first answer is correct. Second-guessing yourself can lead to mistakes and waste valuable time. If you're unsure, take a deep breath, trust your preparation, and stick with your initial answer.

- o **Tip:** If you've learned the concepts thoroughly, you can be more confident in your choices, minimizing the need for second-guessing.

4. Watch Out for Common Pitfalls:

- o **Misreading the Question:** Carefully read each question and all options before answering. Some questions may contain keywords like "not" or "except" that can change the meaning of the question.

- o **Ignoring Instructions:** Pay attention to special instructions. Some questions may have specific instructions, such as selecting more than one option or answering based on a particular scenario.

- o **Overlooking Answer Choices:** For multiple-choice questions, don't choose an answer too quickly. Sometimes, one option may seem correct at first glance, but another answer may be more complete or accurate.

Effective Study Strategies for the CCNA Exam

1. **Create a Study Schedule:**
   - Plan your study time in advance to ensure you cover all the key topics. Break your study into manageable chunks and set specific goals for each session.
   - **Tip:** Dedicate time each week to review and reinforce weak areas, and set aside at least one or two days for mock exams and revision in the weeks leading up to your exam date.

2. **Understand the Exam Objectives:**
   - Review the official **CCNA exam objectives** published by Cisco. The exam will test your knowledge on key areas such as IP addressing, routing, switching, network security, and automation. Make sure you understand each topic, and don't just memorize commands— understand how and when to use them.
   - **Tip:** Break down the objectives into smaller, more digestible sections and tackle them one at a time.

3. **Hands-On Practice:**
   - Practice is key to passing the CCNA exam. Use tools like **Cisco Packet Tracer**, **GNS3**, or real

hardware to practice setting up and troubleshooting networks. Hands-on experience will reinforce theoretical knowledge and help you retain important concepts.

- o **Tip:** Set up your own labs with real-world scenarios, such as configuring VLANs, routing protocols, and ACLs, to gain practical experience.

4. Use Online Resources:

- o Utilize online platforms, such as **Cisco Networking Academy, YouTube tutorials**, and study forums, to reinforce your learning. Participate in discussions to clarify doubts and share knowledge with fellow learners.
- o **Tip:** Watch videos and read articles from experts to get different perspectives on difficult topics.

5. Practice with Real CCNA Exams:

- o Take practice exams to familiarize yourself with the types of questions that may appear on the actual CCNA exam. This will help you gauge your progress, identify weak areas, and get accustomed to the exam format.
- o **Tip:** Do at least **3-5 practice exams** before the actual exam day. Focus on improving time management and learning from your mistakes.

6. Review and Reinforce Your Knowledge:

- o After each study session, spend a few minutes reviewing what you've learned. Use flashcards, quizzes, and practice problems to reinforce your understanding.
- o **Tip:** Make a list of key concepts and review them regularly. The more you revisit the material, the more confident you'll feel when answering questions on the exam.

7. **Don't Cram Last Minute:**

- o Cramming the night before the exam is not effective for CCNA preparation. Instead, spend your last few days reviewing your notes and refreshing your memory on key topics.
- o **Tip:** Focus on reinforcing core concepts rather than trying to memorize everything. On exam day, aim for mental clarity and confidence.

8. **Stay Healthy:**

- o A well-rested mind performs better in exams. Ensure you get enough sleep during your study periods and take breaks when needed. Stay hydrated, eat well, and keep stress under control.
- o **Tip:** On exam day, have a healthy breakfast and avoid last-minute cramming. This will keep your energy levels high and your mind sharp.

Summary

Time management and exam strategy are critical for success on the CCNA exam. By understanding the exam format, prioritizing questions, and using effective study techniques, you can maximize your chances of passing. Implementing strategies like starting with simulations, setting time limits for each section, avoiding common pitfalls, and practicing hands-on labs will help you feel confident and prepared. Combine this with a disciplined study schedule, regular practice exams, and a clear understanding of the exam objectives to increase your readiness. With proper planning and execution, you can approach the CCNA exam with confidence and achieve success.

CHAPTER 23

PRACTICE EXAMS AND TEST PREPARATION

Sample Practice Questions and Answers

Practicing with sample questions is an excellent way to prepare for the **CCNA exam**. Below are sample questions covering a variety of topics you're likely to encounter on the exam. These questions will help you test your knowledge and apply what you've learned.

---

1. IP Addressing and Subnetting:

Question:

You are given the network `192.168.10.0/24` and need to create 4 subnets. What is the subnet mask for the subnets, and what are the first three subnet ranges?

Answer:

- **Subnet Mask:** `255.255.255.192` or `/26` (since we need to divide the original network into 4 subnets).
- **Subnet Ranges:**

o **Subnet 1:** `192.168.10.0/26` (Range: 192.168.10.0 - 192.168.10.63)

o **Subnet 2:** `192.168.10.64/26` (Range: 192.168.10.64 - 192.168.10.127)

o **Subnet 3:** `192.168.10.128/26` (Range: 192.168.10.128 - 192.168.10.191)

---

2. VLAN Configuration:

Question:

You need to configure a switch with two VLANs. VLAN 10 will be used for the sales department, and VLAN 20 will be used for the marketing department. How do you configure VLANs and assign ports on a Cisco switch?

Answer:

- **Create VLANs:**

```arduino
Switch(config)# vlan 10
Switch(config-vlan)# name Sales
Switch(config)# vlan 20
Switch(config-vlan)# name Marketing
```

- **Assign Ports:**

```
arduino

Switch(config)#        interface        range
fastEthernet 0/1 - 10
Switch(config-if-range)#  switchport  mode
access
Switch(config-if-range)# switchport access
vlan 10
Switch(config)#        interface        range
fastEthernet 0/11 - 20
Switch(config-if-range)#  switchport  mode
access
Switch(config-if-range)# switchport access
vlan 20
```

3. Routing Configuration:

Question:

Which command would you use to configure a static route
to the 192.168.20.0/24 network with the next hop of
192.168.1.1?

Answer:

```
arduino
```

```
Router(config)#     ip     route     192.168.20.0
255.255.255.0 192.168.1.1
```

4. Network Security (ACLs):

Question:

You need to configure an access control list (ACL) that denies traffic from the `192.168.10.0/24` network to the `192.168.20.0/24` network while allowing all other traffic. What command would you use?

Answer:

```
arduino
```

```
Router(config)#     access-list     100     deny     ip
192.168.10.0 0.0.0.255 192.168.20.0 0.0.0.255
Router(config)# access-list 100 permit ip any any
Router(config)# interface gigabitEthernet 0/1
Router(config-if)# ip access-group 100 in
```

How to Evaluate Your Progress with Mock Exams

Mock exams are a vital tool for preparing for the **CCNA exam**. They simulate the actual test environment and help assess how well you understand the material. Here's how to evaluate your progress effectively with mock exams:

1. **Time Management:**
   o Use mock exams to practice time management. Make sure you complete the mock exam within the allocated time (120 minutes for the CCNA exam). This will help you pace yourself during the actual exam.
   o If you find yourself running out of time during practice exams, adjust your strategy. Perhaps you're spending too much time on difficult questions or not managing your time effectively across different sections.

2. **Identify Weak Areas:**
   o After completing a mock exam, review your incorrect answers and focus on the areas where you made mistakes. Is there a particular topic that consistently trips you up (e.g., subnetting, routing protocols, VLAN configuration)?
   o Use this feedback to guide your study. Spend more time on areas of weakness, revisiting the theory, and practicing hands-on labs.

3. **Review Performance on Simulations:**
   o Simulations in the CCNA exam test your ability to apply knowledge in real-world scenarios. After

completing mock exams, pay special attention to how well you perform on simulations.

- o Ensure you understand why a particular configuration works and how to troubleshoot network problems. If you struggled with any simulations, recheck your configuration steps and try to identify areas for improvement.

4. **Track Your Improvement:**

- o Take practice exams periodically and track your performance over time. Notice any patterns, such as improvement in certain areas or consistent mistakes. This helps you adjust your study plan to address gaps in your knowledge.

- o **Tip:** Use a **study tracker** to monitor your progress and set goals for improving specific areas each week.

5. **Simulate Exam Conditions:**

- o Make your mock exam as close to the real test as possible. Ensure you take the exam under the same conditions—sitting in a quiet room, using only the resources you'll have in the real exam, and adhering to the time limits.

- o Avoid looking up answers during the practice test. This will give you a more realistic assessment of your knowledge and test-taking skills.

Review of Common Exam Mistakes and How to Avoid Them

While preparing for the CCNA exam, it's essential to be aware of common mistakes and know how to avoid them. Here are some of the most frequent pitfalls and strategies for overcoming them:

1. **Not Reviewing the Exam Objectives Thoroughly:**
   - **Mistake:** Focusing too much on one topic or neglecting other important areas because they seem less familiar or challenging.
   - **Solution:** Always review the **CCNA exam objectives** published by Cisco. This ensures that you cover all the necessary topics and don't overlook critical areas like security, network services, and automation.

2. **Misinterpreting Questions:**
   - **Mistake:** Failing to read questions carefully, especially questions with "not" or "except." This can lead to choosing the wrong answer.
   - **Solution:** Pay close attention to the wording of each question. Always read through each option before selecting an answer. In case of doubt, eliminate clearly incorrect answers and focus on the remaining choices.

3. **Spending Too Much Time on Difficult Questions:**

   o **Mistake:** Getting stuck on a question that you find challenging, causing time pressure later in the exam.

   o **Solution:** If you encounter a difficult question, **skip it** and come back to it later. Focus on the questions you're confident about, and save the challenging ones for the end of the exam.

4. **Not Practicing Enough Hands-On Labs:**

   o **Mistake:** Relying only on theory and not practicing enough real-world configurations.

   o **Solution:** Hands-on practice is critical. Use simulation tools like **Cisco Packet Tracer**, **GNS3**, or real Cisco devices to practice tasks like IP addressing, VLAN configuration, routing, and ACL setup. This practical experience is vital for performing well in simulations on the exam.

5. **Not Reviewing Mistakes:**

   o **Mistake:** Not reviewing the practice exams or labs after completing them, which can lead to repeating the same mistakes.

   o **Solution:** After each practice test or lab, review the incorrect answers thoroughly. Understand why your choice was wrong and why the correct answer is correct. This will help you avoid making the same mistakes on the actual exam.

6. **Ignoring the Simulation Questions:**

   o **Mistake:** Underestimating the importance of the simulation questions and not practicing them properly.

   o **Solution:** Allocate extra time for practice with simulation questions, especially configuration tasks like setting up routing protocols, VLANs, or NAT. These tasks are critical for the exam and can significantly impact your score.

7. **Not Getting Enough Rest Before the Exam:**

   o **Mistake:** Cramming the night before the exam, which can lead to exhaustion and mental fatigue during the test.

   o **Solution:** Ensure you get a full night of sleep before the exam. Resting your mind will allow you to think more clearly and improve focus and performance on exam day.

Summary

Practice exams and mock tests are vital tools for preparing for the **CCNA exam**. They help you assess your knowledge, identify areas for improvement, and build confidence for the actual exam. By simulating the test environment, you can develop a time management strategy and familiarize yourself with the types of questions you will encounter. To maximize your preparation, review your mistakes, adjust your study plan accordingly, and continue practicing hands-on labs to reinforce your skills. Being aware of common exam mistakes and implementing strategies to avoid them will increase your chances of success on the CCNA exam.

Part 6

Beyond CCNA

CHAPTER 24

NEXT STEPS AFTER CCNA

After earning your **CCNA** certification, you've taken the first step in building a solid foundation in networking. However, this is just the beginning of your networking career. There are several pathways you can pursue to expand your knowledge and advance in your career. Let's explore the next steps after obtaining your CCNA, focusing on further certifications, advanced topics in networking, and career opportunities.

Pathways for Further Cisco Certifications (CCNP, CCIE)

1. **Cisco Certified Network Professional (CCNP):**
   - ○ **What it is:** The **CCNP** is the next logical step after the CCNA certification. It builds on the foundational knowledge from CCNA and dives deeper into routing, switching, and troubleshooting.
   - ○ **Exam Structure:** The CCNP certification requires passing several exams that cover advanced topics in network routing, switching,

and security. The exams focus on more complex network designs and configurations.

- For example, **CCNP Enterprise** includes topics like advanced routing (OSPF, EIGRP), VLANs, security, and QoS (Quality of Service).

  o **Skills Learned:** After achieving the CCNP, you will have a deeper understanding of complex networks, including implementing and troubleshooting large-scale enterprise networks, configuring network devices for high availability, and performing more intricate routing and switching tasks.

  o **Career Prospects:** The CCNP certification opens doors to more senior networking positions such as **Network Engineer**, **Network Administrator**, and **Network Architect**. You may also be more qualified for roles that focus on network design and high-level network management.

2. **Cisco Certified Internetwork Expert (CCIE):**

   o **What it is:** The **CCIE** is one of the highest levels of certification in the networking industry. It's intended for individuals who want to specialize in designing and managing large, complex networks.

- o **Exam Structure:** The CCIE certification requires passing both a written exam and a rigorous **lab exam**, which tests practical knowledge in a real-world environment.
    - For example, the **CCIE Enterprise Infrastructure** exam tests advanced routing and switching concepts, automation, and network security.
- o **Skills Learned:** A CCIE professional has expertise in designing, configuring, troubleshooting, and managing networks in complex environments, including working with cutting-edge technologies like SD-WAN and cloud networking.
- o **Career Prospects:** CCIE-certified professionals are considered elite network engineers. They typically take on roles such as **Network Architect**, **Lead Network Engineer**, or **Consultant** in high-demand areas. CCIEs are highly respected in the industry, and their expertise is sought after by large enterprises and global service providers.

Advanced Topics in Networking (SDN, Cloud Networking)

As you advance in your networking career, you'll encounter several emerging technologies and advanced topics that are shaping the future of networking. Here are a few areas to explore after CCNA:

1. **Software-Defined Networking (SDN):**
   - o **What it is: SDN** is an approach to networking that allows network administrators to manage network services through abstraction of lower-level functionality. It separates the control plane from the data plane, enabling centralized network management and automation.
   - o **Why it's important:** SDN allows for more flexible and dynamic networks, with a focus on network automation, security, and scalability. It is especially useful for large-scale data centers, cloud environments, and multi-tenant networks.
   - o **How to Get Started:** To dive into SDN, you can pursue certifications like **Cisco's DevNet Associate** or **Cisco's CCNP Enterprise** (which includes SDN topics in the curriculum).
   - o **Career Prospects:** Learning SDN will open doors to roles such as **SDN Engineer, Network**

Automation Engineer, or **Cloud Network Engineer**.

2. **Cloud Networking:**

   o **What it is: Cloud networking** involves connecting and managing network infrastructure in cloud environments. It integrates on-premises data centers with cloud services (e.g., AWS, Microsoft Azure, Google Cloud).

   o **Why it's important:** As businesses increasingly move their infrastructure to the cloud, understanding cloud networking and how to design and manage networks for hybrid cloud environments is becoming a crucial skill for network engineers.

   o **How to Get Started:** Look into cloud-specific certifications like **AWS Certified Solutions Architect** or **Microsoft Certified: Azure Network Engineer Associate**. Cisco also offers cloud-focused certifications like **CCNP Cloud**.

   o **Career Prospects:** With cloud networking skills, you can pursue roles such as **Cloud Network Engineer, Cloud Solutions Architect**, or **Cloud Operations Manager**.

3. **Network Security:**

   o **What it is:** Network security involves protecting the integrity, confidentiality, and availability of data and networks. Security is an integral part of modern network design and implementation, especially with the rise of cyber threats.

o **Why it's important:** Network security professionals are in high demand as businesses prioritize safeguarding their data and infrastructure. Skills in securing routers, switches, firewalls, and VPNs are critical for maintaining a secure network.

o **How to Get Started:** Cisco offers specialized certifications like **CCNP Security** and **Cisco Certified CyberOps Associate** for those interested in network security.

o **Career Prospects:** Network security knowledge will allow you to take on roles such as **Network Security Engineer, Firewall Administrator**, or **Security Consultant**.

Real-World Career Opportunities for Certified Network Engineers

Cisco certifications, particularly **CCNA, CCNP,** and **CCIE,** can open a wide range of career opportunities in the networking industry. Here are some examples of roles that you can pursue as a network engineer:

1. **Network Engineer:**

o **What you'll do:** As a **Network Engineer**, you will be responsible for designing, configuring, managing, and troubleshooting an organization's networks. This may include managing local area networks (LANs), wide area networks (WANs), and wireless networks.

o **Skills Needed:** Strong knowledge of routing, switching, IP addressing, VLANs, NAT, and network protocols.

2. **Network Administrator:**

o **What you'll do:** A **Network Administrator** manages the day-to-day operations of an organization's network. You'll handle tasks such as monitoring network performance, configuring network devices, and troubleshooting issues.

o **Skills Needed:** Proficiency in network monitoring tools, firewalls, and security configurations. Experience with routers and switches is essential.

3. **Cloud Network Engineer:**

o **What you'll do:** As a **Cloud Network Engineer**, you'll focus on designing and managing the connectivity between an organization's data centers and cloud services. This includes ensuring seamless communication between on-premises infrastructure and cloud resources.

- o **Skills Needed:** Understanding of cloud platforms like AWS, Microsoft Azure, or Google Cloud, as well as hybrid networking concepts, SDN, and cloud security.

4. **Network Architect:**

- o **What you'll do:** A **Network Architect** designs large-scale networks and ensures they meet the organization's business needs. This role involves strategic planning, designing scalable networks, and providing oversight for network performance.

- o **Skills Needed:** Deep expertise in routing, switching, and security. Knowledge of emerging technologies like SDN, cloud networking, and virtualization.

5. **Network Security Engineer:**

- o **What you'll do:** As a **Network Security Engineer**, you will protect network infrastructure and data from cyber threats. This role involves configuring firewalls, VPNs, and intrusion detection/prevention systems (IDS/IPS).

- o **Skills Needed:** Expertise in network security protocols, firewalls, VPNs, and encryption technologies. Knowledge of security compliance standards and risk management.

6. **Network Automation Engineer:**

- o **What you'll do:** A **Network Automation Engineer** focuses on automating network configurations, monitoring, and troubleshooting. This helps organizations improve network efficiency, reduce errors, and streamline operations.
- o **Skills Needed:** Proficiency in programming/scripting languages such as Python, knowledge of SDN and automation platforms, and understanding of network management tools.

Summary

Earning your **CCNA** certification is just the beginning of a rewarding career in networking. After achieving CCNA, you can pursue further Cisco certifications like **CCNP** or **CCIE** to specialize in more advanced networking technologies. Exploring emerging topics like **SDN, cloud networking**, and **network security** can position you as an expert in high-demand areas. Networking professionals are needed in various roles, including **Network Engineer, Cloud Network Engineer**, and **Network Security Engineer**, across industries and sectors. As the networking field continues to evolve, staying updated with new technologies and certifications will ensure that you remain competitive and ready for the future.

CHAPTER 25

NETWORKING IN THE REAL WORLD: CASE STUDIES

Real-World Examples of CCNA Knowledge Applied in Industry

The knowledge gained through **CCNA** certification is widely applicable in various industries and real-world network environments. The following case studies highlight how the core principles learned in CCNA—such as IP addressing, VLANs, routing, switching, and network security—are applied in practice across different sectors.

---

1. Case Study: Small Business Network Design and Implementation

Industry: Small Business

Objective: Design and implement a cost-effective network for a new small business.

Problem: A startup company with 30 employees needs to set up a reliable and secure network for email, file sharing, and internet access. The business requires multiple subnets for different departments (e.g., HR, Sales, and Admin), a guest network, and security measures to prevent unauthorized access.

Solution:

- **IP Addressing and Subnetting:** Using the principles learned in CCNA, the network engineer subnetted the `192.168.0.0/24` network into smaller subnets, providing separate IP ranges for each department and the guest network. The subnets were as follows:
  - o **HR:** `192.168.0.0/26`
  - o **Sales:** `192.168.0.64/26`
  - o **Admin:** `192.168.0.128/26`
  - o **Guest Network:** `192.168.0.192/26`
- **VLAN Configuration:** The engineer configured **VLANs** on the Cisco switch to logically separate the departments. VLAN 10 was assigned to HR, VLAN 20 to Sales, VLAN 30 to Admin, and VLAN 40 to Guest access.
  - o This ensured security by isolating department traffic and limiting access to sensitive resources.
- **Routing:** A **router** was used to enable **inter-VLAN routing** for communication between departments.

Static routes were configured to allow routing between VLANs.

- **Network Security:** The engineer used **Access Control Lists (ACLs)** to restrict access between VLANs (e.g., preventing HR from accessing Sales resources) and set up a **firewall** to secure the network's perimeter.

Outcome: The business was able to have a secure and efficient network that met the requirements for internal communication, internet access, and guest networking. The design ensured future scalability and was easy to manage with clear network segmentation.

---

2. Case Study: Enterprise Network Upgrade

Industry: Enterprise IT
Objective: Upgrade the network to support higher bandwidth, reliability, and security as the company expanded to multiple sites.

Problem: A large enterprise needed to upgrade its existing network to accommodate new data center equipment, remote offices, and cloud-based services. The company faced issues

266

with **network congestion, redundancy**, and **lack of centralized control**.

Solution:

- **Network Redundancy:** Using concepts learned in CCNA, the engineers implemented **dual-homed connections** for each critical network path. **Spanning Tree Protocol (STP)** was used to prevent loops, and **EtherChannel** was configured between switches to provide link aggregation and failover.

- **Routing and Switching:** The engineers upgraded to **Layer 3 switches** for better scalability and faster routing. They configured **dynamic routing protocols** like **OSPF** to ensure automatic route adjustments as the network grew.

- **Wide Area Network (WAN) Design:** The company used **MPLS (Multiprotocol Label Switching)** to connect remote offices securely and efficiently. The engineers also implemented **VPN** solutions for secure remote access.

- **Network Segmentation:** The company deployed **VLANs** for each department and applied **Inter-VLAN Routing** to facilitate communication while keeping departmental traffic isolated for better performance and security.

- **Network Monitoring: SNMP** and **NetFlow** were enabled on Cisco devices for real-time monitoring and traffic analysis, helping the team proactively address performance issues.

Outcome: The network upgrade resulted in better bandwidth management, fault tolerance, and security. The enterprise's distributed offices could securely access centralized data and applications, and the network was easily scalable to meet future demands.

3. Case Study: Cisco Network for a Data Center

Industry: Data Center / Cloud Computing
Objective: Design and implement a scalable, secure, and resilient network for a cloud services provider.

Problem: A cloud service provider needed a network capable of handling multiple customers' data, providing high availability, and offering flexibility for expanding its infrastructure.

Solution:

- **Spine-Leaf Architecture:** Inspired by modern data center designs, the engineers used the **spine-leaf topology** to improve scalability and reduce latency. The spine switches connected to all leaf switches, ensuring minimal congestion in the data center network.

- **High Availability: HSRP** (Hot Standby Router Protocol) was configured for router redundancy to prevent a single point of failure. The leaf switches were connected to each spine switch to ensure link redundancy and availability.

- **SDN Integration:** The engineers leveraged **Software-Defined Networking (SDN)** concepts to automate network management and reduce the complexity of configuring devices. SDN allowed for centralized control over the network traffic, enabling the data center to easily manage customer data flows and provide secure and isolated environments for each customer.

- **Storage Network:** A dedicated **Storage Area Network (SAN)** was set up to provide fast, reliable, and scalable data access for cloud-hosted applications and virtual machines.

- **Security:** The cloud service provider deployed advanced **firewalls** and **IDS/IPS** systems to secure both internal traffic and customer data. **VPN** technologies were configured for secure communication between the data center and remote users.

Outcome: The new network infrastructure enabled the provider to scale quickly, offer enhanced security features, and deliver high-performance services to customers. The design allowed for quick provisioning of new customer networks and ensured high availability, even during peak demand periods.

How Businesses Utilize Cisco Networks

Businesses across various industries utilize **Cisco networks** to address specific networking challenges and meet their organizational goals. Here's how Cisco technology is used in different business environments:

1. **Small and Medium Businesses (SMBs):**
   - SMBs leverage **Cisco switches, routers, and firewalls** to create secure and scalable networks

at affordable costs. Cisco's **small business routers** and **smart switches** allow for easy configuration and management, supporting essential services like email, file sharing, and VoIP.

2. **Large Enterprises:**

   o Large enterprises use **Cisco Catalyst switches, Cisco Nexus data center switches, and Cisco routers** to handle large-scale networking needs. These businesses often deploy **Cisco SD-WAN** for secure and reliable connectivity between remote locations and the data center.

3. **Service Providers:**

   o **Telecommunications and internet service providers** use Cisco's **carrier-grade routing platforms** to deliver reliable and high-speed internet services. **Cisco's Service Provider Routing Technology** supports the transmission of high volumes of data across vast networks.

4. **Educational Institutions:**

   o **Universities and schools** implement Cisco networking solutions to provide high-performance Wi-Fi, secure student data, and enable collaboration tools like video conferencing. **Cisco Meraki** is commonly used for wireless access points, security, and cloud-based network management.

5. **Healthcare:**

   o **Hospitals** rely on Cisco technology to maintain secure, HIPAA-compliant networks for patient data, medical devices, and remote consultation systems. **Cisco Identity Services Engine (ISE)** and **Cisco Umbrella** help protect sensitive information and ensure reliable connectivity.

Lessons Learned from Real-World Network Design and Management

1. **Planning is Key:**

   o A well-thought-out network design ensures scalability, reliability, and security. Understanding business requirements and future growth potential is crucial to avoid unnecessary reconfigurations later on.

2. **Redundancy and Fault Tolerance are Crucial:**

   o Businesses cannot afford prolonged downtime. Ensuring redundancy through **dual-homed links**, **HSRP**, and **load balancing** helps prevent single points of failure.

3. **Security is Not Optional:**

- Implementing network security from the beginning is vital. **Firewalls, VPNs, ACLs**, and **IDS/IPS** systems are essential for protecting sensitive data and preventing cyber threats.

4. **Network Monitoring is an Ongoing Requirement:**
   - Proactive network monitoring helps identify and resolve issues before they impact users. Tools like **SNMP** and **NetFlow** allow for continuous monitoring and traffic analysis, ensuring optimal performance.

5. **Scalability and Flexibility:**
   - Businesses need to design networks that can grow with them. Scalable architectures like **spine-leaf** or **modular networks** allow organizations to add resources and users as needed without complete redesigns.

6. **Documentation and Regular Updates:**
   - Documenting the network configuration, topology, and changes is essential for troubleshooting and future upgrades. Regularly updating the network infrastructure and security policies helps keep the network running smoothly and securely.

Summary

Real-world applications of **CCNA** knowledge demonstrate the importance of sound network design, planning, and management. Businesses in various industries—small to large—rely on Cisco technology to provide secure, scalable, and resilient networks. Whether it's a small business, a cloud service provider, or a large enterprise, **Cisco networking** is a trusted solution to meet their connectivity needs. Through these case studies, we learn that redundancy, scalability, security, and proactive monitoring are essential components of a successful network, while lessons from real-world scenarios reinforce the importance of careful planning and continuous learning.

CHAPTER 26

FINAL REVIEW AND RECAP

Key Takeaways from the Book

As we wrap up this book, it's important to reflect on the essential networking concepts and Cisco knowledge you've gained throughout your CCNA preparation journey. Here are the key takeaways:

1. **Foundational Networking Knowledge:**
   - You've learned the basics of **networking models**, including the **OSI model** and **TCP/IP model**, and how each layer plays a crucial role in network communication.
   - Understanding **IP addressing** and **subnetting** is fundamental to designing networks and troubleshooting IP connectivity.
   - **VLANs**, **routing protocols**, and **switching techniques** such as **OSPF**, **EIGRP**, and **static routing** are essential for building robust, scalable networks.
   - The concept of **network security** using tools like **ACLs**, **firewalls**, and **VPNs** is vital for protecting networks from internal and external threats.

2. **Cisco IOS and Device Configuration:**

- o Mastering the **Cisco CLI** (Command-Line Interface) allows you to configure and manage Cisco devices effectively. You learned how to configure **routers, switches**, and **firewalls** using common Cisco commands and settings.
- o **Routing and Switching**: Key Cisco technologies like **HSRP, VTP, EtherChannel**, and **Spanning Tree Protocol (STP)** help create fault-tolerant, efficient networks.

3. **Advanced Networking Topics:**
   - o You gained exposure to **SDN (Software-Defined Networking)**, **cloud networking**, and **automation**, which are the future directions for networking technologies.
   - o The importance of **network redundancy, failover mechanisms**, and **scalability** were emphasized in both **small and enterprise-scale networks**.

4. **Exam Preparation Strategies:**
   - o The CCNA exam requires both theoretical knowledge and practical hands-on experience. Throughout the book, you practiced troubleshooting, configuring devices, and applied real-world scenarios.
   - o You learned how to approach exams strategically, manage time effectively, and

understand key topics to focus on for optimal preparation.

Final Exam Tips and Last-Minute Study Advice

As the CCNA exam approaches, here are some last-minute tips to help you maximize your chances of success:

1. **Review Key Concepts:**
   o Focus on **IP addressing, subnetting, VLANs, routing protocols**, and **network security**. These topics make up a large portion of the exam and are foundational to many of the questions.
   o Revisit **Cisco CLI commands** for configuration and troubleshooting. Make sure you are comfortable with commands related to VLAN setup, routing protocols, and network security.
   o Brush up on **network troubleshooting skills**. Practice identifying network issues based on symptoms and using the appropriate Cisco commands to fix them.

2. **Practice, Practice, Practice:**
   o Take **practice exams** to simulate real test conditions. This will help you get familiar with the question format and improve your time management.

o Spend time in **hands-on labs**. Use tools like **Cisco Packet Tracer, GNS3**, or physical routers and switches to configure and troubleshoot networks.

o Focus on **performance-based questions (PBQs)**, as these require you to demonstrate practical skills. Practice configuring networks, troubleshooting, and responding to real-world scenarios.

3. **Don't Cram:**

o Avoid cramming the night before the exam. Ensure you get a good night's sleep so you're well-rested and alert.

o Instead of trying to memorize everything, focus on understanding the concepts. The CCNA exam is designed to test your ability to apply knowledge, so understanding the "why" behind each concept is critical.

4. **Time Management During the Exam:**

o On exam day, pace yourself by answering easier questions first. Skip difficult questions and mark them for review.

o Don't get bogged down by one question. If you're unsure, make your best guess and move on.

o Keep an eye on the clock to ensure you have enough time for each section. Allocate extra time for simulations and leave the last 10-15 minutes for review.

How to Stay Up-to-Date with Cisco Technologies and Networking Trends

The world of networking is constantly evolving, and staying up-to-date with new technologies and industry trends is crucial for maintaining and advancing your skills. Here are a few ways to stay informed and continue your learning journey:

1. **Follow Cisco's Official Resources:**
   - **Cisco Learning Network:** The Cisco Learning Network provides forums, study groups, and resources related to Cisco certifications. It's an excellent place to connect with other networking professionals and stay informed about the latest Cisco technologies and updates.
   - **Cisco Blogs and Webinars:** Cisco regularly publishes blogs, whitepapers, and webinars about new products, technologies, and trends in networking, cloud, security, and automation.
2. **Participate in Industry Events and Conferences:**

- o Attend industry conferences such as **Cisco Live**, where Cisco showcases its latest innovations, provides technical training, and offers networking opportunities. Cisco Live is an excellent platform for learning about new certifications, products, and networking trends.

- o Participate in online forums and communities like **Reddit's /r/networking** or **Network Engineering Stack Exchange**, where networking professionals share knowledge and discuss emerging technologies.

3. **Explore Advanced Certifications:**

- o After CCNA, continue to pursue advanced Cisco certifications such as **CCNP** (Cisco Certified Network Professional) or **CCIE** (Cisco Certified Internetwork Expert). These certifications will expose you to cutting-edge topics like **Software-Defined Networking (SDN)**, **Cloud Networking**, and **Network Automation**.

- o Explore **Cisco DevNet** for certifications in network automation and programming, which are growing fields in network engineering.

4. **Follow Industry News and Innovations:**

- o Stay informed about trends in **cloud computing**, **network automation**, **SD-WAN**, **5G networking**, and **IoT** (Internet of Things). These areas are significantly shaping the future of networking.

- o Subscribe to networking magazines or newsletters such as **Network World** or **TechTarget**, which offer valuable insights on the latest networking technologies and best practices.

5. **Engage with Networking Communities:**

- o Join LinkedIn groups, Discord communities, or local meetups dedicated to networking professionals. These communities offer insights, job opportunities, and discussions on the latest trends.

- o Join **Cisco DevNet** to learn about network automation and APIs, which are transforming how networks are managed.

6. **Hands-On Experience:**

- o Continue practicing in **Cisco Packet Tracer**, **GNS3**, or real lab environments to test your knowledge of new features and technologies. Experiment with automation tools, SDN protocols, and cloud configurations to stay ahead of the curve.

Summary

Achieving **CCNA** certification is an important milestone, but it's only the beginning of your journey in networking. By reviewing key concepts, practicing extensively, and applying time management techniques, you can pass the exam with confidence. After the CCNA, further certifications like **CCNP** or **CCIE** will expand your expertise and open up more career opportunities. To stay up-to-date with the ever-evolving world of networking, continue learning through Cisco resources, participate in industry events, and keep practicing hands-on labs. Networking is a dynamic and exciting field, and staying current will help you remain competitive and advance your career.